jetlag travel guide

Phaic Tăn

SUNSTROKE ON A SHOESTRING

Hardie Grant Books

First published in 2004
by Hardie Grant Books in conjunction with Working Dog Pty Ltd

Hardie Grant Books
85 High Street
Prahran Victoria 3181
Australia
www.hardiegrant.com.au

text © Working Dog Pty Ltd 2004
photos © photographers 2004 (see p4)
maps & illustrations © Working Dog Pty Ltd 2004

The National Library of Australia Cataloguing-in-Publication Data:
Cilauro, Santo.
Phaic Tan: Sunstroke on a shoestring.
ISBN 1 74066 110 9.
1. Wit and humor, Pictorial. 2. Travel writing – Humor. 3.
Parodies. I. Gleisner, Tom, 1962– . II. Sitch, Rob. III.
Title.
A827.4

JETLAG ™   ™ Phaic Tan ™

www.jetlag.com

10 9 8 7 6 5 4 3 2 1

Qac!

[Welcome!]

Written by Santo Cilauro, Tom Gleisner & Rob Sitch
Cover and text design by Trisha Garner
Maps by Bruce McGurty, Paul de Leur & Astrid Browne
Printed and bound by Tien Wah Press [PTE] in Singapore

ILLUSTRATIONS :
Bill Wood: 18, 20, 23, 27, 28–9, 32, 45, 61, 67, 102, 116, 144–5, 172–3, 208–9, 245
Trisha Garner: 43, 70, 139 **Costa Constantinou**: 60 **Milo Angel**: 64, 65, 85 **Michele Burch**: 25

PHOTOGRAPHY (in alphabetical order) :
Tony Adamson & Kathryn Henderson: 6, 45, 50, 78, 87, 97, 150, 195, 198, 206, 211,
220, 235, 246, 255 Sean Boyle: 32, 52, 77, 123, 168, 185 **Michele Burch**: 14–15, 66, 70,
73, 75, 80, 143, 150, 151, 170–1, 174, 175, 181,186, 225, 255, **Grand Master William
Cheung**: 62 **Debra Choate**: 7, 8, 54, 66, 67, 108 **Adam Haddrick**: 14, 33, 52, 53, 57, 230,
242, **David Herman**: 6 **Fiona Herman**: 19, 76, 108, 136, 148–9, 155, 187, 195, 197, 219,
230, 236, 244 **Celia Hirsh**: 77, 247 **Freda Hirsh**: 56, 70–1, 223, 226, 245 **Michael Hirsh**:
26, 53, 96, 107, 109, 112, 119, 137, 190, 205 **Paul Leslie**: 171 **Lonely Planet:** 11, 93,
120, 138, 232–3, 254 **Jason McNamara:** 53 **Nicole Mandile:** 48–9, 58, 87, 109, 121, 122,
147, 149, 215, 240 **Susannah Mott**: 7 **Leandro Palacio**: 188 **Tracey Prince**: 16, 191 **Marty
Rudolph**: 46, 52, 87, 168, 176, 177, 198–9, 246 **Emmanuel Santos**: 10, 13, 15, 16–17,
24, 30, 35, 36–7, 41, 52, 54, 58–9, 60, 68, 78, 79, 80, 82, 89, 91, 102, 105, 108, 123,
134, 137, 141, 146, 148, 157, 166, 174, 176, 184, 192, 194, 198, 222, 228, 230–1,
232, 234, 247, 248–9 **Rob Steer**: 3, 11, 12, 14, 16, 18, 22, 25, 31, 35, 38, 54, 55, 56,
63, 70, 72, 72–3, 77, 80, 83, 90, 97, 101, 105, 110, 113, 167, 200–1, 203, 223, 224,
227, 228, 229, 232, **Working Dog** (Santo Cilauro, Tom Gleiser, Rob Sitch): 6, 7, 8, 9, 10, 15,
17, 19, 21, 24, 30, 31, 34, 36, 37, 38, 39, 42, 44, 47,49, 50, 51, 52, 53, 55, 59, 71, 72,
73, 74, 76, 79, 80, 81, 82, 83, 84, 87, 91, 92, 93, 94, 95, 96, 98, 100, 101, 103, 104,
106, 107, 110–1, 112, 115, 118, 119, 121, 122, 124, 125, 127, 128, 129, 132, 133,
135, 138, 139, 140, 142, 146, 147, 152, 159, 165, 170, 175, 178, 185, 187, 194, 196,
199, 200, 204, 207, 221, 224, 231, 233, 237, 241, 243, 244, 255, 256, **Yvan Cohen/
Asiaworksphotos.com**: 86

COVER PHOTOGRAPHY
Front cover (clockwise from top left): **Adam Haddrick** (main portrait), **Celia Hirsh** (background
to portrait), **Working Dog**; Front flap: **Marty Rudolph**; Inside front cover: **Bill Wood**; Inside back
cover: **Working Dog** (*Arduous Walks of the World*) **David Herman** (*Travel for Seniors*) **Rob Steer**
(*International Tax Havens*) **Michele Burch** (*Let's Go Game Hunting*); Smiling man on front
cover: **Emmanuel Santos**

THE AUTHORS WOULD LIKE TO THANK:
Kirsten Abbott, Tony Adamson, Milo Angel, Daniel Atkins, Fran Berry, David Brian, Michele
Burch, Grand Master William Cheung, Kim Choate, Richard Cobden, Costa Constantinou,
Neale & Sharina Delves, Dolly & Joe Dunstone, Elizabeth Ellmer, Trisha Garner, Sandy Grant,
Hardie Grant Books, Kathryn Henderson, Fiona Herman, Alex Hill, Will Houghton QC, Jane
Kennedy, Ray Kennedy, Legends – South Yarra, Martine Lleonart, Daniel McCoppin, Therese
McCoppin, Jason McNamara, Susannah Mott, Mary Muirhead, Mark Nelson, Brian O'Donohoe,
Julie Pinkham, Billy Pinnell, Shaun Risse, Emmanuel Santos, Greg Sitch, Evelyn Snow, Thomas
Snow, Frankie Sonnenberg, Mark Stewart, Strike – Nicole Hamilton, Polly Watkins, Bill Wood.

Contents

01 Getting Started

02 Bumpattabumpah

03 Thong On

04 Pha Plung

05 Sukkondat

Contributors

Graeme and **Diane West** were born in London where they worked as teachers before travelling overseas to Southeast Asia. Together they wrote *Baby Abroad*, *Family Odyssey* and the hugely popular *Have Kids – Will Travel!* They divorced in 1998.

Sean Beauford grew up in New Zealand where he worked as a flying instructor before visiting Phaic Tan for the first time in 1996. Since then he has made many return trips to the country's east, drawn by both a love of the region and a desire to find the missing members of his family.

Dr Roberta Oricoli heads the editorial section of Jetlag Travel. An experienced writer and holder of a doctorate in comparative linguistic semiology, she was in charge of prove reading this book.

Sandra Tait has travelled extensively around the world and currently lives in Maine with her husband Brad, also a Jetlag writer. An intensely private couple, little else is known about the pair except that Brad suffers from erectile dysfunction.

Sophie Le Cal has trekked and lived extensively throughout Asia and the Pacific region. Most recently she spent several months travelling round Bangkok after becoming stuck on the city's Sky Rail. In 2002, her article *Fine Dining in Phaic Tan* won a Global Traveller award for 'Best Work of Fiction'.

Markus Christoff first visited Phaic Tan as a volunteer field worker for an international aid agency. Struck by the rural people's trusting nature, he decided to stay and set up a business selling basic agricultural equipment at greatly inflated prices.

Jenny Ronalds is a freelance travel writer with a special interest in Southeast Asia who, over the years, has contributed numerous articles to *Travel & Leisure*, *Globe Trotter* and *International Gourmet*. None have ever been published and we kind of felt sorry for her.

Andrew Cootes was born in North Dakota. An expert on security and counter-terrorism, Andrew has provided advice on travel safety to both the U.S. and British governments. In 2003 he was caught providing advice to a North Korean government official and now lives in a single bedroom apartment at Guantanamo Bay.

Maree Van Eyck was just a teenager when her parents first moved to Southeast Asia and it took her almost three years to track them down. Since then she has been living in Bumpattabumpah where she teaches English. Maree is the author of *What Parasite is That? A Guide to Phaic Tanese Street Food*.

Aaron Clarke originally travelled throughout Asia working on community aid projects before returning home to New Zealand where he completed a degree in theology. A respected pastor, he writes regularly for *The New Christian* as well as numerous other evangelical publications. Aaron helped compile our section on Phaic Tan's sex industry.

Feature Contributors

This Jetlag Guide also features contributions from some of the most experienced and opinionated travel writers in the world, each an expert in his or her field. Look out for Top Tips from...

PHILIPPE MISEREE
For the genuine travel experience...
Philippe has been travelling for his entire life and prides himself on having visited just about every place in the world at least twice; once to experience it and then again a few years later to be disappointed by the changes.

' *In researching this book, I discovered a myriad of beautiful beaches and breathtaking sights. I'm quite sure you will not find as many and if you do, remember – I was there first.* '

TINA PAYNE
Better safe than sorry...
On Tina's first trip to Europe almost 20 years ago she suffered food poisoning, had her luggage stolen and was physically assaulted within two hours of arrival. Even though the person responsible was subsequently arrested (it turned out to be her husband), the experience left an indelible mark and prompted Tina to write several popular books, including *The Cautious Traveller*, *Security Abroad* and the international bestseller *Stop! Thief!*

' *Hotel room doors can be notoriously flimsy and their locks easy to pick. Whenever staying overseas I barricade the door, remove all light bulbs from their sockets and sleep in a set of night vision goggles.* '

SVEN TEITARSSEN
Dollars and sense...

A devoted backpacker, budget traveller and author of *The World on a Shoestring*, Sven has crossed the globe whilst barely spending a cent. An acknowledged expert on internet specials, stand-by rates, concession card deals and shoulder season discounts, his determination to travel cheap is so great that on one recent trip through Southeast Asia he actually made a profit.

' *Travellers eating out on a budget can often take advantage of early bird specials. Having your evening meal at 11.30 in the morning can shave up to 40% off the bill. Bring your own plastic cutlery and negotiate further discounts.* '

JONATHAN QUIBBLE
For the luxury traveller...

Jonathan is a self-confessed *connoisseur*, *bon vivant* and *user-excessif* of the French language who specializes in top-end travel. Jonathan can – and will – find fault in even the finest five-star hotel or award-winning restaurant. Presenter of the popular TV series *Unaffordable Travel*, Jonathan's books include *Overpriced Villas*, *Fine Dining Around the World* and *Travelling with Gout*.

' *The resort was beautifully designed and the service trés exceptional. If I had to make one criticism, the wine list – at just 117 pages – was a little limited for my tastes.* '

Note *Before the publication of this book Jonathan suffered a massive heart-attack, one that he described as 'similar to my last three'. He is currently on leave awaiting quadruple bypass surgery.*

Rhai Sing Dhamp

The fertile **SUKKONDAT** *province – where happy farmers harvest hay in order to camouflage their primary crop, opium.*

Pong

River

Kui

KHOU

Prahtaprohng

PALAHN

Sloh Phan

SUKKONDAT

Gunsa Wah
2150m

Kwong Teng

CHIUNG

Mong Qoc

Nahkthong

MAI SHLONG

MOK

Prohm Tenh

THONG ON

Duq Xang

Stong Phraht

Mt Siyuden
1507m

Sombor Palan

Ka
Tr

River

The exotic **THONG ON** *province – a beach-lover's paradise, where sea meets souvenir shop.*

Pattaponga

RD

Trong Bai

GREAT

AIC TAN

*Kru Kut
Bay*

Pt Taken

Prohp Kang

NAHKTHONG
DELTA

Nahkthong

Khravat Is

Ban Mi Is

NONG

Mawlung
Is

Talok Pruohm

Meggaprahng

PH

Na Chok Is

Khapak Is

STRAITS

Koh
Samosa
Is

Phra Salahng

Pt Lefreq

LHONG CHUK SEA

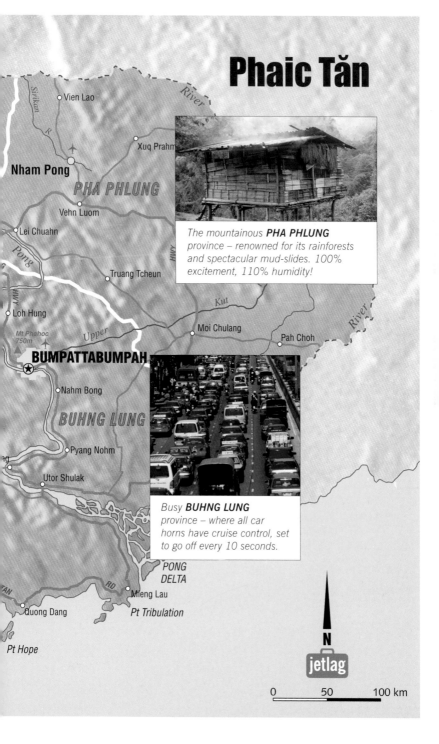

Phaic Tăn

Vien Lao

Sirikan

River

Xuq Prahm

Nham Pong

PHA PHLUNG

Vehn Luom

Lei Chuahn

Pong

Truang Tcheun

HWY

*The mountainous **PHA PHLUNG** province – renowned for its rainforests and spectacular mud-slides. 100% excitement, 110% humidity!*

Kut

Loh Hung

Upper

Moi Chulang

Pah Choh

River

Mt Phahoc
750m

BUMPATTABUMPAH

Nahm Bong

BUHNG LUNG

Pyang Nohm

Utor Shulak

*Busy **BUHNG LUNG** province – where all car horns have cruise control, set to go off every 10 seconds.*

PONG
DELTA

Mleng Lau

Quong Dang

Pt Tribulation

Pt Hope

N

jetlag

0   50   100 km

Traditional boatmen (Pyrehts) await customers on Phaic Tan's magnificent Kra Vat Coast.

A Portrait of Phaic Tan

For the first-time Western visitor, a trip to Phaic Tan can be a genuine assault on the senses – an overwhelming explosion of sights, sounds, tastes, smells and strange colonic movements. But most agree that once you spend some time in this **tropical paradise** it has a strange way of getting into your blood.*

Peace at Last

Sadly, for far too long, the very name Phaic Tan has come to be associated with atrocities, poverty and bloodshed. This, combined with sub-standard duty-free **shopping opportunities**, has understandably limited the number of travellers visiting the country. But after years of bitter conflict, Phaic Tan is finally a nation at peace, with armed hostilities now confined to just a few northern provinces and the Bumpattabumpah Casino. Throughout the land citizens – who for years served in **underground militia units** – have at last downed their weapons and are now welcoming overseas visitors with an open arm.

Land of Contrasts

Phaic Tan is truly a beguiling land of contrasts, where **traffic police** wear face masks but surgeons rarely do, a country where littering is an indictable offence yet landlords may legally use torture to extract overdue rent, a nation that boasts the world's highest number of amputees per head of population yet, paradoxically, has never won a medal at the Para Olympic Games.

Visitors to Phaic Tan also vary widely – from the ubiquitous backpacker drawn by the lure of untouched tropical beaches and 24-hour **foot massage facilities** – to the discerning luxury traveller keen to indulge in some of the world's most exclusive coastal resorts, **five-star retreats** so luxurious that staff are sacked daily just to maintain freshness.

Such is the magic of Phaic Tan that many who come, intending to stay for a week, never manage to leave (see our section on Narcotics – Penalties for).

Phaic Tan boasts some of the lowest lying land in Southeast Asia. Here a typical family celebrate the arrival of the Dry Season.

* For more information, see our section on Typhoid.

Phaic Tan is now making its mark on the international stage. The world's number one exporter of cocktail umbrellas and disposable chopsticks, Phaic Tan was recently named as host nation of the 2006 Southeast Asian Hackey-Sack Championships.

Something for Everyone

There's something in Phaic Tan for everyone. History buffs will adore the many ruins – temples, palaces, public hospitals – that dot the country. Nature lovers won't want to miss catching a glimpse of the rare Irrawaddy **freshwater dolphins** inhabiting many eastern rivers (see our section on Game Fishing Charters). If you're a sun-seeker, venture west to the beach resorts of Thong On where you can lounge by a pool or snorkel out to the spectacular **artificially coloured reef**. And if adventure tourism is your thing, head for the heavily de-forested jungles of the north for some '**brown-water rafting**' where adrenalin-junkies can surf one of the largest mud-slides in Southeast Asia.

Of course, fans of **fine dining** won't be disappointed either. Phaic Tanese cuisine can best be described as 'explosive', a fiery combination of chilli, garlic and pepper to which food is occasionally added. Whether you dine at a five-star restaurant or a simple street vendor's stall, the memory of these meals will stay with you long after the **intestinal parasites** have been eradicated.

Moves to improve Phaic Tan's air quality by regulating industry and cracking down on the illegal burning of rainforest have met with only partial success. There are, however, plans to limit the number of mosquito coils that may be lit to one per family per day.

The People

But for all its natural attractions, many believe that it is the Phaic Tanese people themselves who are the 'star attraction'. Imbued with a **curious blend** of politeness and militant Maoism, they have staged some of the most courteous revolutions in Asian history. Indeed, these friendly, **outgoing folk** clearly value good manners above all else. Rarely will you hear a raised voice or terse remark between locals. In fact, it's not unusual to see two drivers, having been involved in a collision, get out of their vehicles and exchange gifts. Here, **cultural diversity** and racial tolerance abound, with Malays, Chinese, Thai, Laotians, Khmer and Burmese living side by side in detention camps while, on the other side of the **razor wire**, native Phaic Tanese go about their business.

With one foot in the past and another striding determinedly forward, Phaic Tan truly is a nation going in circles.

HEALTH NOTE Visitors to Phaic Tan should rest assured that there have been no new reported cases of SARS (Severe Acute Respiratory Syndrome) or reports of Avian Flu since last year when the Government launched a mass eradication program to rid the country of all journalists.

Hot, humid and covered in lush vegetation, it's little wonder that Phaic Tan is often described as being 'the armpit of Southeast Asia'.

01

Phaic Tăn
Getting Started

A Look at the Past

Archaeologists believe that Phaic Tan was once a **major thoroughfare** for Neanderthal man en route from Africa to Asia. While the more developed members of this migratory group continued through, the slower, **smaller-brained specimens** settled in Phaic Tan and began reproducing. Initially tree-dwellers, as the forests receded they were forced into evolutionary change. Many came down and spread out across the plains where they flourished. A small sub-group attempted to live underwater and quickly died out. Evidence of **rice cultivation** as early as 4000BC has been found in the north-east of the country, with historians unearthing primitive agricultural equipment as well as an extremely ancient bottle of **soy sauce**.

At the end of the second millennium BC, bronze, brass, pewter and jade were brought to the country by **Chinese immigrants**. The people of Phaic Tan were quick to realize the potential of these new metals and opened what is believed to be Asia's first ever souvenir shop.

Modern civilization did not become established in Phaic Tan until about two thousand years ago, when waves of people from central and southern Asia migrated here, drawn by the abundance of food and **child-care facilities**. It was around this time that the wheel was introduced. A short while later the people started using numbers and, not long after that, roulette was invented.

By about the seventh century merchants and **missionaries** from India began to arrive. The merchants introduced new political and social values, along with art and architectural values from the west. The missionaries introduced bingo. Around this time the Tubom, a renegade sect of **militant Buddhist crusaders** from Burma, invaded the country and the people of Phaic Tan had non-violence forced upon them.

HOMO DISORIENTATUS
How this one-million-year-old African man came to be found in Southeast Asia remains a mystery.

MYOPIARAPTOR
Fossilized remains of this dinosaur have been found just east of Nham Pong. An extremely short-sighted creature, it actually developed a two foot thick skull after a millennia of running into trees.

The Age of Kings

The first man to unite Phaic Tan was King Ahamthibodi (b. 1113?) who established the country's capital in Dhing Dhong after a **stunning victory** over the Chinese in what is now referred to as the Great Dhing Dhong Battle. King Ahamthibodi initiated splendid architectural achievements (the giant Waterslide of Nha Trang was built by him in 1135) and developed the modern Phaic Tanese written language, an **elegant cursive script** modelled on serrations of the palm frond. His glorious reign only came to an end in 1141 after an ill-advised and highly unpopular attempt to introduce daylight savings into the country's south.

An early portrait of King Ahamthibodi. The artist was subsequently executed.

Next came the kingdom of Prejedhipok ('Preji the Bold') who shifted the capital west to the coastal settlement of Hop Siep where he established Phaic Tan's first **Eternal City**. The Eternal City was burnt to the ground the following year and then re-built, only to be flooded, decimated by an **earthquake** and buried under a series of landslides, eventually prompting Prejedhipok to abandon the concept of an Eternal City. But during his reign he oversaw the construction of many capital works, culminating in the glittering palace of Miahm.

This **glorious monument** (*left*) was built entirely of gold and silver tiles that reflected the sun with such brilliance it was said the light could be seen 200 kilometres away. King Prejedhipok lived here until 1189 when he was forced to leave due to **retinal damage**.

The Heavenly Spire at the Palace of Miahm stands 154m in height (155m counting the TV antenna).

In 1963 archeologists working in the southern village of Khuam Lo unearthed an ancient stone panel on which were inscribed numerous carvings, many of a sexual nature, accompanied by lewd inscriptions. Historians now believe this to be one of the oldest public lavatory doors ever found.

Emperor Khai Huong

The longest reigning ruler in early Phaic Tanese history, Emperor Khai Huong came to power during the mid 13th century. A **gifted philosopher** and religious scholar, he is credited with formulating the maxim 'all life is suffering', after a **wet weekend** spent listening to his son practise the clarinet.

But despite his longevity, Khai Huong's reign was plagued by misfortune: his palace burnt down frequently, the royal elephant 'Thrunc' died after developing an allergy to peanuts and, despite having 104 wives, this noble ruler was lucky to manage sex once every second month.

In 1650 the Dutch established the Dutch East India Trading Company in western Java to exploit **spices** found in various parts of the archipelago. Sadly, it turned out that Phaic Tan had little to offer in the exotic spice department apart from *rsangabaa*, a bitter derivative of the yewtel tree widely used throughout Europe as a means of keeping snails off **ornamental gardens**. Despite this, the Dutch stayed and attempted to impose colonial rule until their fleet was routed on August 11, 1678 in what came to be known as the 'Night of the Floating Clogs'.

In 1690 the French invaded and a series of **bloody battles** were fought. Greatly outnumbered, Phaic Tanese troops were forced into retreat, eventually taking refuge in the eastern city of Lhaym Dhuc. It was here, facing almost certain defeat, that their commanding officer General Prishav Katachburi urged his men to commit *au-chi wau-chi*, or **honourable suicide**, telling them that by dying in battle they would reach a state of nirvana. Another officer pointed out that by not dying in battle they could reach the mountains, at which point over 4000 Phaic Tanese troops downed weapons and headed for the hills. With French troops massing outside his palace, Phaic Tan's ruler Prince Tay-Sun made one last attempt to stave off defeat by re-naming himself Pierre François and wearing an I♥PARIS T-shirt but it was too late.

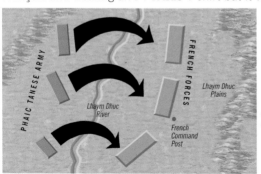

Phaic Tanese warrior carrying the traditional attack arrow.

The failed Phaic Tanese assault on French Forces in the battle of Lhaym Dhuc.

Struggle for Independence

The French then went on to rule for almost 200 years, and their legacy remains to this day in Phaic Tanese architecture, fashion and a 12% service charge throughout the hospitality industry. In 1797 a **mass uprising** led by Kundrup Phung, a young peasant farmer from the north, temporarily drove the colonial government out. Phung immediately bestowed upon himself the title of Emperor Dewak Akung 'Lord of Lords' – although he was known to palace officials as 'Shorty' – and set about the task of re-unifying his country. Emperor Phung ruled wisely for over two decades but towards the end of his reign began suffering from **paranoia** – he had monks killed, along with his own wife and children. His ministers were eventually forced to get rid of him – he was swiftly kidnapped, covered in a velvet sack and beaten to death with a sandalwood club. In certain parts of Phaic Tan this process is still regarded as a **traditional welcome**.

Something of a power vacuum then ensued, with two cousins of the former Emperor locked in a battle for the throne. The older cousin, Lhong Moh challenged his rival Buhm Phluph to a duel, with weapons of his own choice. The next morning at dawn the two men faced each other with **wet towels**. Lhong Moh won the contest and went on to rule for over 30 years.

Modern History

King Mok Mai Shlong led Phaic Tan into the 20th century as a semi-independent nation, establishing an effective civil service, formalizing **global relations** and having the country formally admitted to FOPN (Federation of Opium Producing Nations).

During the 1920s Phaic Tan was wracked by a bitter civil war, eventually forcing the Government to divide the combatants by constructing a **massive wall** running from Hhumok in the west to Phop Kra on the eastern plains. An enormous architectural undertaking, the wall spanned just over 300km; however, being made of **rice paper screens**, it was frequently breached.

HUAN KRO KUP

Early last century, this brilliant but little known mathematician fused differential calculus and risk analysis with numerology to prove that '3' is the unluckiest of unlucky numbers. Incredibly he died on 4/4/44.

WWII

With the commencement of World War II, Phaic Tan chose to side with the Japanese after Royal Astrologers predicted an **easy victory**. At the end of the war no punitive measures were taken against Phaic Tan, although the Chief Astrologer was transferred to **house-keeping duties**.

By this stage Phaic Tan was a **constitutional monarchy** with power shared between the King (Divine Rule) and the Military (Heavily Armed Rule). All too often Phaic Tanese governments were plagued by corruption, prompting frequent uprisings. In one week during the spring of 1948, 117 separate attempts to overthrow the government took place, forcing parliament to implement their strict '**One Coup Per Family**' policy.

The Fight for Freedom

Post-war was a difficult time for human rights in Phaic Tan as the Government fell under control of the **hard-line** right wing Prime Minister Tuph Nhut. His **autocratic rule** led to the formation of numerous underground rebel groups, including the People's Liberation Alliance (KPZ), the Phaic Tanese Freedom Fighters (ATA) and the Democratic Rights Brigade (DRB) – the first anti-government group whose acronym bore any resemblance to its name. The struggle for **civil rights** found its most common expression in frequent student uprisings that were often met with violent treatment from the army. The low

point came in September 1951 when troops opened fire on a mob of kindergarten students. This outrage led to **mass riots** and protests the following week in the capital Bumpattabumpah where a group of communist rebels seized control of the radio station and declared a revolution. They also declared it 'No Repeat Tuesday'. The Houses of Parliament were stormed and the Government overthrown in a **bloodless coup**, all Ministers being strangled.

Prime Minister Tuph Nhut, known as the 'Short-sighted Visionary', seen here taking a break during the Peasants Purge of 1953.

The American CIA has had a chequered history of undercover involvement in Phaic Tan. During the 1960s they launched 'Operation Restore Democracy', a covert plan to install a military junta. This was followed by 'Operation Freedom', a plan to replace the junta with a single dictator which, in turn, led to 'Operation Enduring Friendship' – three months of constant carpet bombing.

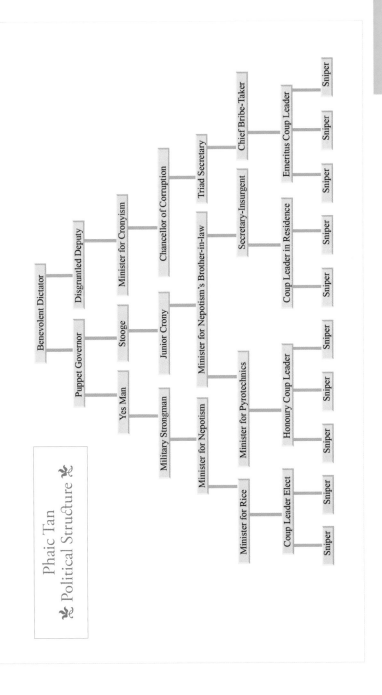

Phaic Tan
❧ Political Structure ❧

TREAD CAREFULLY...
It's important to remember
that Phaic Tan is still littered
with UXO, or unexploded
ordinance. Much of these can
be traced back to the civil wars
of the 1960s and 70s although
an alarming proportion appear
to be a result of the 2000
New Year's Eve celebrations.
Despite on-going attempts
to clean up the problem,
UXO continue to be a very
real threat and, as recently
as just last year, four people
were being maimed each
day. Interestingly, it was the
same four people, determined
– if somewhat foolhardy
– members of a Phaic
Tanese bush-walking club.

*People caught planting
land mines now face
heavy on-the-spot fines.*

Civil Unrest

With the country on the brink of all-out civil war
and numerous groups claiming a mandate to
govern, interim Prime Minister Chan Tuxay took
charge of a 24-party **coalition government** who
spent the next year building a cabinet table large
enough for them to all sit round. Chan Tuxay was
forced to stand down in 1955 after **unexpected
surgery** – his leg was shot off by insurgents
– and the country looked set for further turmoil.
Fortunately, former Prime Minister Chu Kondoc
was persuaded to return from retirement and take
over as Head of State.

Debate continues as to whether the 103-year-old
statesman was really up to the job or even aware of
where he was. At the **swearing-in ceremony** the
only phrase he uttered was 'you're not the nurse'.

Constitutional Reform

Despite this, Chu Kondoc managed to unite Phaic Tan
and oversee its first **Bill of Rights**. Borrowing heavily
on a badly translated US version, this document
guarantees – amongst other things – all citizens 'the
right to bare arms', the only time **short-sleeved
shirts** have received constitutional protection.

*Traffic police in Phaic Tan are quite tough when it
comes to road rules and transgressing tourists may
find themselves issued with an on-the-spot bribe.*

'Closed Door' Policy

Between 1965 and 1980 Phaic Tan hibernated in a long period of **isolationism**. Little contact was made with the west and no foreign imports were allowed into the country, other than the Government purchasing the first and second series of *Happy Days*. As a result, many Phaic Tanese children born during this period are still called 'Phonzi'.

Tiger Economy

Recent years have seen stability return to Phaic Tan, but recovery from the **Asian economic crisis** of the late 90s has been slow. The International Monetary Fund currently puts Phaic Tan's foreign debt at $4.2 billion – much of this figure relating to travel expenses wracked up by current Prime Minister Khou Palahn who, despite strict **austerity measures**, insists on journeying to Parliament each week from his home in St Moritz.

The Present

Of course, Phaic Tan is not a country without its problems. Government corruption remains an issue, as does **organized crime** and social injustice. Even today young girls are being kidnapped from city brothels and taken to country villages where they're forced to work as teachers. But slowly things are improving and the future looks bright for this tropical jewel.

REBEL ROUSER

Many of the student uprisings of the 50s were led by Goh Ti (1932–56), a radical democracy pioneer who believed in the power of mass protest. Addressing a rally in his home-town of Ayuthach, he declared that nothing could stop the people if they stood united. At this point in the speech he stood on a table and was decapitated by a ceiling fan.

Goh Ti discusses politics at a rally in 1951.

After five decades of political upheaval, in 2004 the Government officially adopted a new national slogan: 'Phaic Tan – Under New Management'.

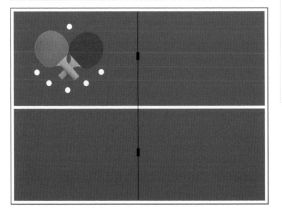

(Left) Phaic Tan's national emblem, the Pihng Pohng, is quite unusual – being the world's only hinged flag. Whilst unconventional, it does make flag-folding ceremonies more efficient.

Royal Family

The Royal Family holds a special place in the hearts of all Phaic Tanese people and any sign of disrespect towards them will be viewed unfavourably. This fact was brought home just a few years back when a foreign visitor who made anti-royal remarks was asked to step off a Phaic Tanese Airways plane, despite the fact it was at 33,000 feet above the Andaman Sea.

His Majesty

The current king is His Majesty Sukhimbol Tralanhng III, ninth king of the **Angit dynasty**. A well travelled and much loved monarch, in times of crisis such as war or military coups the people of Phaic Tan have always turned to him. And even though he could rarely be found, preferring to hole up in a Swiss chateau until the danger passed, this has in no way diminished his reputation as a wise and **trusted leader**. Interestingly, King Tralanhng prides himself on being something of a musician and composer. In fact, the country's national anthem (the *Rong Ki*) was actually written by him and whenever it is played Phaic Tanese will immediately stand and respectfully place one hand over each ear. Regular performances of King Tralanhng's **jazz works** are held at the palace and it is considered an enormous honour to be forced to attend. Sadly, the King's health has declined in recent years and not long ago Royal Physicians advised that he should stop playing the saxophone. The date of this pronouncement has since been declared an **unofficial national holiday**.

Kitchen hands at the Royal Palace individually search fortune cookies for any messages that may be deemed critical of the King or his family.

Her Majesty

King Tralanhng's wife is known as Her Royal Highness Queen Suahm Luprang. Also much loved and revered by the people of Phaic Tan, Queen Luprang does have something of a **temper**, especially when it comes to unflattering photographs of herself.

In 1995 the country's second biggest newspaper was shut down after it published a picture of Her Majesty that could, from certain angles, have led loyal subjects to believe she had a **double chin**. The photographer responsible, along with editorial staff, is now serving time at a re-education facility.

HEIRS TO THE THRONE Crown Prince Ferduk is the King's eldest son and therefore next in line to the throne. The Prince is a keen sportsman who actually won an athletics gold medal in the 100m sprint event, despite being well back in the field, at the recent Asia-Pacific Games when the other competitors were all arrested without warrant. Intelligent and well educated, Prince Feruk spent several years in the USA at Harvard University, where he failed to gain a degree but did gain quite a reputation as a 'pants man'.

Next in line to the throne is **Princess Buk Phang** who, despite years of orthodontic treatment and extensive cosmetic surgery, still shares her mother's striking looks. Known as 'the People's Princess', she is rarely seen in public.

The youngest member of the Royal Family is **Prince Luat** ('Luat the Brooding') who, unfortunately, made headlines a few years ago when he walked into the palace during a state function armed with a semi automatic pistol and opened fire. Mercifully, due to Luat's extreme short-sightedness he failed to hit a single family member; however, the Royal Dog sustained serious leg wounds and had to be eaten. Shortly after, Prince Luat was committed to Phaic Tan's newest psychiatric hospital, named in his honour.

Royal Palace

The Royal Palace in Bumpattabumpah is considered to be one of the finest examples of early Phaic Tanese architecture and attracts thousands of tourists every day. Completed in 1680, this magnificently ornate landmark took over 75 years to build, although much of this time was spent getting the plans through council.

Ornamental Pond

The Tallest Wat in Asia
This sumptuously decorated, tiered spire has been struck by lightning so many times that it is now permanently connected to the country's main electricity grid.

The People's Hall
(Closed to the public.)

The Southern Wing
Relocated in 1938 by feng shui advisors to the Palace's western side.

Old Moat Used once a year as a street circuit for the Formula 1 Grand Prix.

Inner Wall Several of the murals along this section have been attributed to the famous monk-painter Dhekam Wharyam, although the drawing of a naked woman at the eastern end is believed to be the work of grafitti vandals.

The People's Park
(Closed to the public.)

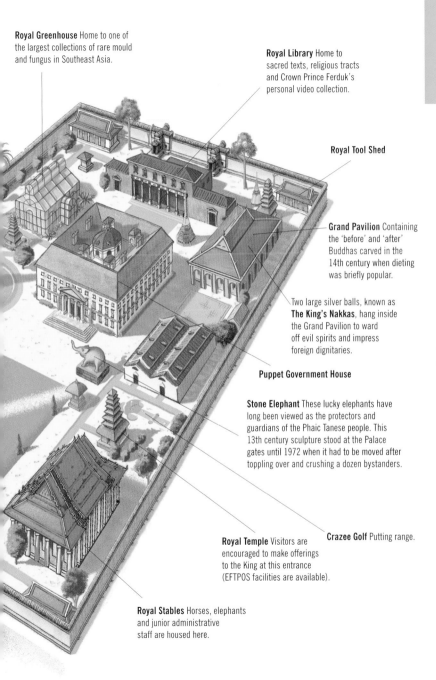

Royal Greenhouse Home to one of the largest collections of rare mould and fungus in Southeast Asia.

Royal Library Home to sacred texts, religious tracts and Crown Prince Ferduk's personal video collection.

Royal Tool Shed

Grand Pavilion Containing the 'before' and 'after' Buddhas carved in the 14th century when dieting was briefly popular.

Two large silver balls, known as **The King's Nakkas**, hang inside the Grand Pavilion to ward off evil spirits and impress foreign dignitaries.

Puppet Government House

Stone Elephant These lucky elephants have long been viewed as the protectors and guardians of the Phaic Tanese people. This 13th century sculpture stood at the Palace gates until 1972 when it had to be moved after toppling over and crushing a dozen bystanders.

Crazee Golf Putting range.

Royal Temple Visitors are encouraged to make offerings to the King at this entrance (EFTPOS facilities are available).

Royal Stables Horses, elephants and junior administrative staff are housed here.

The People

When it comes to its people, Phaic Tan is a true melting pot where, for centuries, the population has absorbed a wide range of ethnic influences. In more recent times they have absorbed a wide range of heavy metals, the result of unregulated copper mining, all of which contribute to the unique national character.

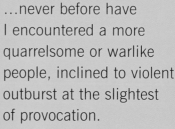

...never before have I encountered a more quarrelsome or warlike people, inclined to violent outburst at the slightest of provocation.

Written in 1712 by a visiting anthropologist Jules Grenouille, shortly before he was stabbed to death by a novice monk angry at the noise Grenouille's pen was making.

There is no denying that the Phaic Tanese have had a long history of bloodshed and violence. In an attempt to kerb these **warlike tendencies**, the Government experimented some years back with adding **oestrogen** to the nation's water supply, a move that resulted in a slight drop in violent crime rates but a massive increase in the formation of **book clubs**. The scheme had to be abandoned, however, when a 37-year-old fireman from Pattaponga took out first prize in the Miss Phaic Tan **beauty pageant**.

Population

It is difficult to know precisely how many people live in Phaic Tan as, being a **Buddhist country**, many citizens are inclined to list both present and past lives when completing population surveys. In addition, more than 300 officials involved in collecting the last **government census** are still missing, presumed kidnapped, so figures are necessarily incomplete.

Overpopulation in some of the larger centres remains a problem and in recent times authorities have embarked on various schemes to reduce the number of people living in Phaic Tan. In 1980 the road speed limit was raised to 340km/h and **pool fencing** was declared illegal, measures that had some immediate success. Population numbers were further reduced in 1992 with the re-introduction of **lead-based petrol**.

Despite changes brought by tourism and commerce, the Phaic Tanese people remain deeply traditional and distinction according to sex is quite stringent. In Phaic Tanese society only the women may tend cattle, cultivate the fields, gather provisions, chop wood, make handicrafts and raise children. Men are expected to prepare sacrifices to the gods and put the bins out.

The Phaic Tanese have an extraordinary ability to fall asleep in public places. This practice is enshrined in their afternoon siesta or khonk, *usually taken between 2 and 4pm.*

Greetings

The **traditional greeting** is the *kop*. To perform this, place your hands together at chest level as if you are praying. Bow your head sharply, taking care not to poke your own eye out (considered a sign of great disrespect), and lean your upper body to the left. You are then in a position to carry on a conversation or perform a **Viennese waltz**.

Various forms of the kop

| GENERAL GREETING | TO ELDERS | TO DIGNITARIES | TO AIRPORT SECURITY |

CRYING POOR…

There's no denying Phaic Tan is a poor country and over recent years numerous international aid agencies (or NGOs) have set up operations here. Some of these organizations, such as the Red Cross and World Vision have prospered while others have struggled, prompting the formation of a new aid agency, 'Aid Aid', established to help struggling aid agencies.

(Right) As well as a greeting, the kop *may be used as a form of self-defence.*

Forms of the *Kop*

The person of lower social status initiates the *kop*. If unsure, attempt to determine the person's social status by their clothing or standard of dental care. To avoid embarrassment, some Phaic Tanese like to carry a copy of their latest **income tax assessment** prominently displayed. In general, you should not *kop* to children or someone you don't know such as a waiter or **armed assaillant**. Also, don't expect a monk to return a *kop* as they are often short-sighted. How low one should bow depends on the social standing of the superior party. If planning to greet a person of extremely high rank it may be necessary to take a **pilates course**.

Saving Face

As with many Asian cultures, the concept of 'saving face' is extremely important to the Phaic Tanese. People will go out of their way to avoid **confrontation and embarrassment**, even if this means saying 'yes' to something that is clearly not possible. In fact, there is not an actual word for 'no' in the Phaic Tanese language, perhaps explaining why every **political referendum** has returned a 100% 'yes' vote. Rather than say 'no' – and thus lose face – Phaic Tanese people will employ a range of euphemisms such as:

- 'Maybe tomorrow'

- 'Certainly not impossible'

- 'Perhaps in the fullness of time'

- 'Yes'

Criticism should always be delivered very carefully. Never tell your cab driver he is going too fast. Simply wait for an opportune moment – such as when you've overtaken on a **blind corner** and are about to slam head-on into a **petrol-tanker** – then casually remark, 'Your driving is of excellent quality; however, I would not be unhappy if greater time were to elapse between the start and fiery finish of our journey.'

When approaching a door with a Phaic Tanese host, they will invariably gesture for you to go first. The **correct protocol** is to politely refuse and attempt to usher your host through. This will generally be greeted by mild protestations and possibly tears at which point a **heated verbal clash** will break out, often followed by a fist fight. Such conflict is considered a great sign of respect, especially if blood is drawn. After both parties have regained consciousness you may proceed through together, but only with some show of reluctance.

WEIGHT GAIN CLINICS

The people of Phaic Tan have the lowest body fat percentage in the world, which explains the large number of businesses advertising themselves as Weight Gain Clinics. The fact is, for many local people being thin is considered undesirable, a sign of poverty, and they will go to considerable lengths to put on bulk. Various techniques are employed, such as calorie-uncontrolled diets, exercise avoidance programs and padded jeans (below), although some desperate Phaic Tanese are resorting to surgical procedures such as lipo-pumping in which fat and cellulite deposits from specially bred pigs are injected into the patient.

Rites & Rituals

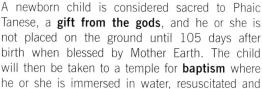

Baptisms

A newborn child is considered sacred to Phaic Tanese, a **gift from the gods**, and he or she is not placed on the ground until 105 days after birth when blessed by Mother Earth. The child will then be taken to a temple for **baptism** where he or she is immersed in water, resuscitated and blessed again. Interestingly, Phaic Tanese children are not actually named until they are one year old (although at three years of age they may legally take charge of a motor vehicle). Most children are not weaned until the age of 14 and for some visitors the sight of a teenage boy attached to a middle-aged woman's breast can be a little off-putting, especially when the two of them are not actually related.

FESTIVALS

On just about any week of the year the Phaic Tanese people will be celebrating a religious or cultural festival of some sort. These include:

Independence Day – from March 1st each year the people spend a week celebrating the fact they are no longer bound by the laws of France, Holland, China, England or the Geneva Convention.

The Pattaponga Monkey Festival – held each May, this is believed to be one of the longest-running culinary events in Asia.

Festival of the Hunt – June/July. Marking the unofficial start of the poaching season, this is not so much a festival as a crude attempt to dignify a widespread, illegal practice.

Vishwang Talang – a week-long celebration of Nham Pong's history and architecture, this festival culminates with locals laying candles at the foot of the city's Vishwang Wat, followed by a procession of fire brigade vehicles attempting to extinguish the resulting blaze.

Phuja – similar to Ramadan or Lent, during October local Buddhists punish themselves by fasting, self-flagellation and attending performances of traditional Phaic Tanese dance.

Procession of the Jet Skis – held on the island of Ban Mi each year to herald the summer renting season, the major jet ski hire companies roar past the Tourism Minister at full throttle in one of the shortest and loudest festivals in the world.

Christmas Day – December 25

Kick Boxing Day – December 26

New Year's Eve – the major Phaic Tanese day of celebration on which fireworks, flares and rocket-propelled grenades fill the air.

Weddings

These are joyous occasions, often lasting for several days. The bride and groom will both wear a veil, to protect against **mosquitoes**, and meet at the temple where offerings are made to the gods and the caterers in hope of happiness. The groom will then present his bride-to-be with a butterfly. She will pull its wings off, considered good luck for all (except the butterfly). After the ceremony the happy couple are showered in **sticky rice**.

In Phaic Tanese weddings it's traditional for the couple to exchange spectacles.

Funerals

Until not so long ago traditional Phaic Tanese funerals involved the deceased being placed on a **ceremonial raft**, set on fire and floated downstream on the nearest river or canal. But the scarcity of firewood combined with a recent incident in which a funeral pyre nearly set fire to a **floating market** has led to a crack down on this practice.

IT'S ACADEMIC
Phaic Tanese parents place great value on education and their children are often under enormous pressure to do well academically. Rather than bring shame on the family, many students who fail to achieve top marks have taken their own lives, a trend that tragically culminated in 1997 with the mass suicide of an entire primary school class.

DRESS SENSE One thing you'll learn quickly in Phaic Tan is that just about everyone has an official dress of some description and wandering the streets you'll come across a bewildering array of insignia, badges and hats. That man in a blue shirt and white helmet is likely to be a traffic cop. Khaki pants, green shirt and whistle generally signify an army officer. Black boots, red gloves and truncheon – he may well be an obstetrician. The fact is, the Phaic Tanese love their uniforms and everyone from street sweepers to undercover agents working for the Phaic Tanese secret service will insist on some form of formal attire.

Etiquette

Western visitors should constantly remind themselves that Phaic Tan is a very **conservative country**. Here women ride motorcycles side-saddle. For many, marriage is consummated in a similar style. Obvious displays of affection such as holding hands, caressing or **fondling** in public should be avoided as they are likely to draw attention, especially if you're on your own.

DID YOU KNOW?
In Phaic Tan it is considered rude to look people in the eye after the original hello. This tendency to avert one's gaze is given as a reason for the repeated failure of local television chat shows.

Dress Code

Dress modestly at all times and avoid any form of clothing that might be considered inappropriate or offensive, such as revealing tops or **safari suits**. Be extra conservative when visiting mosques or temples. Short revealing skirts and **exposed midriffs** on women are frowned upon. Short revealing skirts and exposed midriffs on men is asking for trouble.

Traveller's Tip

The left hand is considered unclean and should never be used to point, unless you are pointing to the toilet.

Remember that women should never try to shake hands with or even hand something directly to a monk. Monks are not permitted to touch women, although some older members have a more liberal interpretation of this sacred edict.

Footwear

An important **etiquette tip** is to always remember to remove your shoes before entering a private home. This not only shows **respect** for the owners, it protects their carpet which often tends to be of very poor quality.

Footwear should also be removed before entering a temple although visitors are warned about the growing incidence of **shoe theft** in some of the larger cities. If your footwear is reported stolen and then recovered you may be required to attend the nearest police station and identify it by sight or smell.

In Phaic Tanese society the head is considered the most sacred part of the body, and the feet are the lowliest. Therefore, do not casually touch another person's head and don't sit with your feet pointing at someone else. Under no circumstances should you touch your own head with your feet.

POINT TAKEN
As in many Asian cultures, it is considered rude to point with the finger. If you need to indicate a direction or signify something, do so with a series of sharp pelvic thrusts that will generally get the message across.

CHAU DHOWN *CEREMONIES*
You won't travel far in Phaic Tan without coming across one of these – a traditional ceremony in which participants sit in a circle and share barok *(rice wine). It is considered an honour to be invited to participate in a* Chau Dhown *ceremony and the ritual can last for several hours, involving chanting, praying, singing and – in recent times – video games. A blue ribbon tied around all celebrants' wrists is to be worn for the next three days, ensuring good luck as well as half price entry into all city nightclubs.*

Religion

Phaic Tanese culture cannot be fully appreciated without some understanding of **Buddhism**, which is followed by 90% of the population. Buddhism was brought to the country in the 13th century by Pud Bhayar, a revered **holy man** who spent years solving the great mysteries of birth and death, only to be stumped by the mystery of sea-monkeys. Phaic Tanese Buddhism is a curious mix of **spirituality and martial arts**. Many religious statues depict Phaic Tanese deities clutching a set of **nunchukas**. Adherants believe in the Four Simple Truths that lead to the Eightfold Path known collectively as the Thirteen Ways. (Maths is not a highly prized part of this belief structure.) Not as strict as some devotees, Phaic Tanese Buddhists follow a **moderate regime** of fasting, prayer and good works; they are, for example, permitted to meditate in front of the television, provided the sound is turned down. The ultimate goal of Buddhists is to detach oneself from the world and reach a state of nirvana or, failing that, Bangkok.

In Phaic Tan people can 'make merit' not only by giving alms or joining the monkhood but also by selling Amway.

Considered one of the holiest sites in Phaic Tan, Wat Kamphun was long said to house relics of Buddha himself, a claim only disproved in 1998 when UN weapons inspectors discovered stockpiles of low-grade uranium stored within.

A common misconception is that all Buddhists are **vegetarians**. The truth is, Buddhists may eat animals – they just can't be responsible for killing them. Hence it is not uncommon to see Phaic Tanese beef farmers herding their cattle along **unfenced cliff-tops** or allowing them to graze in mine fields during violent electrical storms.

What Buddhism all really comes down to is **harmony**. Phaic Tanese believe everything should be in harmony. Good balances evil. A volcano erupts and kills thousands, its ashes provide fertile fields for future generations. There is no pleasure without pain – as anyone listening to a Phaic Tanese **musical recital** will attest.

NATIONAL SERVICE
All Phaic Tanese men must serve two years either in the army or as a monk. For those unable to decide, there is a combination service, the King's Mounted Meditation Corps, one of the world's only military units to go into action with unloaded weaponry.

HOLY CHILD

Wan Dvaravati (1287–1326) is generally considered one of Phaic Tan's holiest teachers. Born in the north of the country, he lived a happy and uneventful existence until the age of seven when his parents demanded he attend school. At this point Wan realized the futility of daily struggle and decided to pursue a life of prayer, meditation and very little housework. Statues of this junior mystic often show him in a reclining position which is pretty much how he spent the next decade, lying on his parent's couch seeking enlightenment. A strong believer in karma, Wan taught those around him that happiness could only be obtained by performing acts of 'merit', such as giving him alms or breakfast in bed. It was during this period he formulated his own **Four Simple Truths**.

1. Suffering comes from the self.

2. Material possession corrupts.

3. My sister's a brat.

4. If she comes into my room again I'll kill her.

Offerings and vows to the gods may take many forms, including flowers, soft drinks and, in some cases, I.O.Us.

Correction *In our last edition we described the Khoa Lak Temple (right) as 'one of the most revered' holy sites in Phaic Tan. It is, in fact, one of the most 'repaired'.*

Monks

All young Phaic Tanese men are expected to enter a monastery for a short period in their life, usually after finishing school, and families earn great merit when one of their sons becomes a monk. Traditionally the length of time spent in the monastery is three months however these days it is possible for Phaic Tanese teenagers to 'earn their robe' in a shorter period. Some less reputable monasteries even offer **correspondence courses** that allow apprentice monks the option of practising either self-denial or the guitar, although these are frowned upon by traditionalists.

Upon first entering the monastery, Phaic Tanese monks live a life of strict meditation and denial, designed to isolate them from the distractions of the outside world. Why, then, so many monasteries appear to have **satellite TV dishes** on their roofs remains a mystery.

Holy Life

After an initial period of study and prayer, young monks may go out into the community but even here holy life is quite **strictly regulated**. According to monastic discipline, novices may only eat once a day – before noon – and must eat only what is in their **alms bowl**. This no doubt explains why Phaic Tanese monks can often be seen carrying alms bowls the size of **large woks**.

Phaic Tanese monks do not earn an income, surviving instead on gifts provided by believers or being paid to chant. In this sense there is a fine line between 'living a holy life' and '**busking**'.

If you want to catch a glimpse of Phaic Tanese monastic life, remember that the **daily alms round** takes place shortly after dawn, when monks leave the temple to search for their daily meal. For most this involves knocking on doors, although increasingly these days young city-based novitiates can be seen lining up for an Egg 'n' Bacon McMuffin.

DRAWING ON THE DIVINE

During the middle ages Phaic Tan's monks were renowned as skilled calligraphers and thanks to their efforts hundreds of sacred texts that could have been lost were faithfully reproduced and preserved. But the process was enormously time-consuming and led to one visionary monk Sri Bhod Kuham (1198–1243) coming up with a quicker method. Using an ingenious combination of wires, ink dispensers and paper holders, he managed to build a prototype of the modern photocopier. It was successfully trialled in 1242, producing four identical images before suffering what is believed to be the world's first ever paper jam.

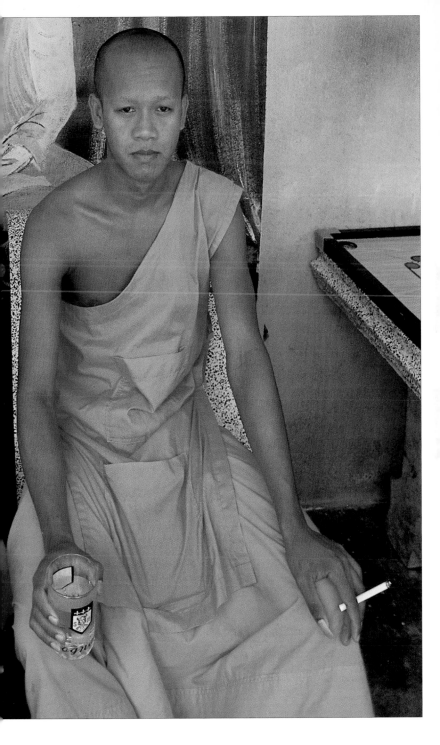

IT'S A FUNNY OLD GAME The Phaic Tanese obsession with lucky numbers is most evident when playing the local billiard game Siamese Pool (*Qic Pot*). Instead of the traditional 15 balls there are only 11 – the '3' and all multiples of '3' are considered taboo. The only exception is the '9', which is a square number, therefore lucky (so much so, that in some areas there are two 9s – the 8 being wrapped in rice-paper and thrown into a mirror). You'll also note that because 6 is a multiple of 3, there are only 5 pockets – the bottom left is stuffed with a bundle of silk – silkworms having 8 legs which is considered extremely lucky. Because the triangle is a 3-sided figure, the balls are arranged in a square. The table must also be on a slant of no greater than 13 degrees.

The numbers 4 and 11 are considered extremely auspicious.

Superstition

There's no denying that Phaic Tan is a land of superstition where fortune-telling, astrology and numerology still play a large role in daily life, influencing everything from wedding dates to **air traffic control**. Even today, people cling to a wide range of non-scientific beliefs about 'sacred' numbers and 'auspicious' dates. In the north of the country it is still considered unlucky to be trodden on by an elephant.

Good Luck

Amongst those things considered lucky in Phaic Tan are: gold fish, jade, the numbers 12, 37 and 4189, not contracting cholera, the colour green, **winning lottery tickets** and sheep. The letter 'a' is considered particularly auspicious and on each full moon homage is paid to the divinity Raaachmaaakaaaamanaaan.

Birth Dates

Phaic Tanese consider it extremely unlucky to be born in certain months and **pregnant women** going into labour at the 'wrong' time may often attempt to delay delivery for up to four weeks. Local midwives have even developed a special set of **forceps** designed to keep a baby's head from emerging.

Golden Opportunity

Men will often touch a blonde-headed child because it is believed to bring gold. They will also touch the **breasts** of a blonde-headed woman because it is believed to bring pleasure.

Of course, it's all very well for westerners to mock such unscientific convictions but it pays to keep an open mind. Even sceptics have been amazed at the unerring accuracy with which **fortune-tellers** can predict how much money their accomplice will steal from your unwatched bag.

Reflexology

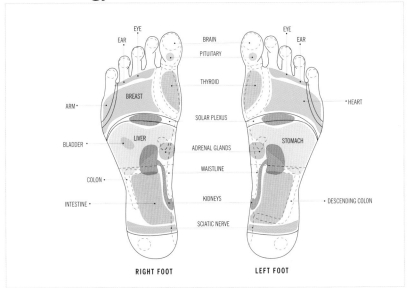

The Phaic Tanese place enormous faith in reflexology (above), so much so that local mechanics are able to identify and treat automotive ailments simply by touch (below).

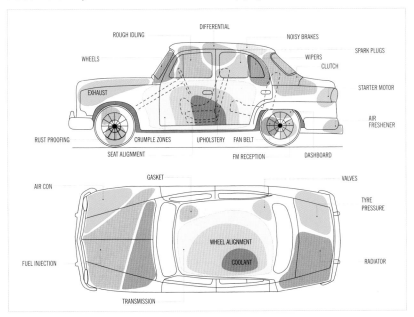

Note Recent attempts to repair flat tyres using acupuncture have met with limited success.

Language

Phaic Tanese is one of the fastest spoken languages in the world – on average, 192 syllables per minute.* Virtually impossible to lip-read, native Phaic Tanese speakers routinely complete their country's entire National Anthem in under 10 seconds. To make matters even more challenging, the Phaic Tanese language is **tonal** and one word can have many meanings depending on the intonation used: 'ha', for example, can signify 'horse', 'tree', 'cloud', 'peace', 'afternoon' or 'you're standing on my foot' – all depending on the pitch and force with which it is uttered.

Spoken Phaic Tanese employs four basic tones: high, low, rising and falling. A fifth tone has emerged in recent years, but this is used primarily by rap artists.

Due to these complexities many **westerners** are reluctant to even try and speak Phaic Tanese. This is a pity as the local people will appreciate enormously any attempt to master their tongue as they really don't have much else to laugh at. And, while some may dissolve into fits of **hysterical giggling** as you attempt the simplest of phrases, take comfort from the fact that many Phaic Tanese children don't manage complete sentences until they are teenagers.

Philippe Writes..

I laugh at people with their phrasebooks stumbling to conjugate verbs and keep up with the simplest of conversations. If you're not prepared to take three months off before a trip to master a language (like me), then don't bother going.

Gender Issues

One of the major difficulties facing **non-native speakers** is that words are not determined by the gender of the person addressed but by the gender of the speaker and the direction he or she is facing. On top of this, sentences can end with a variety of different suffixes (*kar, lo, phar* etc.) depending on the time of day. To further complicate matters, the Phaic Tanese language employs three different levels to indicate the caste or status of the listener, ranging from 'High Phaic Tanese', a formal style full of **elaborate phrases** and rhetorical flourishes, through to 'Low' or 'Common' Phaic Tanese which basically involves **spitting**.

* *Ironically, Phaic Tanese horse-racing callers are amongst the slowest in the world.*

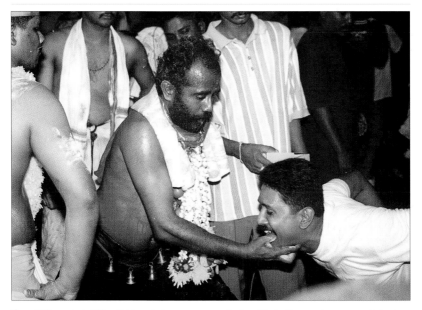

The famous Khmar Kaoling tablet was instrumental in helping to decipher ancient Phaic Tanese dialects. One of the most complex of all ancient scripts, linguists have worked out the series of symbols (above) translates roughly as 'Beware of Dog'.

One of the most difficult sounds to pronounce in the Phaic Tanese language is known as the 'qck' dipthong and even native speakers attempting it may often require immediate physiotherapy.

Food & Drink

If you aren't familiar with Phaic Tanese cooking, imagine the best of Chinese food ingredients prepared with the sophistication of Indian spicing and presented with the **culinary flair** of the finest French restaurant. Of course, the key word here is 'imagine', as the local dining scene in Phaic Tan has suffered from the deprivations brought about by years of warfare and **economic turmoil**. But in recent times Phaic Tanese cuisine has undergone something of a **renaissance** and some exciting treats await the adventurous, digestively robust diner.

Hot 'n' Spicy

There's no denying the Phaic Tanese like their food hot, with chillies being a major part of everything from curries and **stir-fries** through to breakfast cereal and sorbets. In fact, Phaic Tan's version of bon appetit (*'minh laum'*) literally translates as 'may beads of sweat form on your brow'. But the influx of tourists has softened local attitudes and gone are the days when, if a diner requested something 'less spicy', the chef would burst from the kitchen armed with a meat cleaver and **challenge your manhood**.

Apart from chillies, other basic ingredients used widely in Phaic Tanese cuisine are shellfish, vegetables, fruit, bean sprouts, bamboo shoots, lemongrass (or, in poorer regions, lemons in grass), basil, mint and rat.

Visitors won't go far without coming across Sambal sauce, a **firey concoction** of shallots, turmeric, onion, ginger, garlic and red peppers, used widely in both restaurants and homes where it is often given to babies suffering from colic. Another popular condiment is *praherk*, a **pungent-smelling** fish paste used to disguise the taste of certain foods. Unfortunately, nothing can disguise the taste of *praherk* and it is **best avoided**. The most commonly served dish in the north of Phaic Tan is *phoar*, a clear broth or soup traditionally eaten with chopsticks, which could explain the high incidence of malnutrition in this part of the country.

MONKEY BUSINESS!

One of the more bizarre dining experiences you are likely to come across, especially in the hill country of Phaic Tan's north, is fresh monkey brain. Not one for animal lovers, this dish involves removing the skull of a recently killed monkey, ape or adulterer and scooping out the brains which are eaten warm on a bed of lettuce! The dish has its origins in ancient times when cannibal tribes such as the Horhk would attack their lowland neighbours the Mohn people and feast on their brains. Whilst a great ritual the meal sizes simply proved inadequate and so the practice switched to primates.

Traveller's Tip

Protect yourself in restaurants by saying, *Houy mai farater, po!* ('Not spicy! Foreigner!') whilst pointing 👍 to your (or your partner's) bottom.

A Phaic Tanese chef prepares a traditional dish of smoked carp.

Many Phaic Tanese restaurants will offer diners a jug of water. This is not meant to be drunk, it's there to help put out the kitchen should it catch fire.

Festive Food

During times of celebration such as New Year or the cessation of **civil war**, the Phaic Tanese love to serve a special duck dish called *guoman*. The bird is plucked, rolled in spices and slowly roasted over **hot coals** before being brought to the table and killed. Of course, anywhere in Phaic Tan a truly **authentic dining experience** can be had simply by eating at one of the many roadside food stalls. Few of these establishments have menus and so it is often easiest to simply look at what other patrons are eating. If there are no other patrons or they appear to be doubled over in the gutter you might think about moving on.

Fast Food

Remember also that when eating out in Phaic Tan you may at times feel a little rushed to finish your meal. This is because in many restaurants the **traditional emphasis** is not so much on food quality as efficiency. Staff pride themselves on having patrons seated, fed and presented with the bill in under 12 minutes. Diners attempting to 'linger' may often find lights being switched off, chairs stacked and floors mopped around them. Do not be offended.

Dog Food

You won't travel far in Phaic Tan without coming across a restaurant or street stall selling dog. While many foreigners are appalled by this practice, the Phaic Tanese think nothing of it and serve their four-legged friends up in a **dazzling range** of culinary creations. If you do order dog (*lah-see*) you're likely to be presented with its liver, barbecued hind legs, spicy shoulder sausage or minced intestines. Diners unable to finish their meal may take the left-overs home in a **doggy bag**, often made out of the animal's stomach.

DOG GONE IT!

Many western visitors to Phaic Tan are terrified of the possibility that they may – even accidentally – end up eating dog. A good test when served any roast meat is to look closely at the animal's head. While pigs and goats will traditionally have an apple stuffed in their mouth, dogs tend to be cooked holding a tennis ball.

Tina Writes...
For the Cautious Traveller

Food poisoning is a constant risk when eating out overseas. But you can minimize the chances of picking up a nasty bug by taking a packet of surgical wipes and insisting that your chef scrub up before ordering. If you're still not confident, demand all staff complete a food-handling course the day before you arrive.

Fruit Feast

Being in the tropics Phaic Tan naturally produces a **wonderful variety** of fruit, including banana, coconut, papaya and mango. But the most widely grown crop, and one **unique** to the country, is the *salak* – a pungent, slightly oily fruit covered in sharp spikes. The flesh is **inedible** but the spikes are frequently used as toothpicks.

Of course, for something even more exotic, you can't go past the durian. Do not let the **odious smell** of this fruit deter you. Let the taste do that.

Hygiene Standards

Food hygiene standards vary across the country, from poor in the big cities to almost **non-existent** further afield. With fruit and vegetables, follow the **old adage**: boil it, cook it, peel it and then throw it away.

A market vendor asks a customer to sign a legal waiver before selling her produce.

Sven Writes...
For the Budget Traveller

Phaic Tan would have to be one of the culinary capitals of the world and everywhere you go the smell of freshly cooked meat, exotic spices, fragrant rice dishes and succulent seafood fills the air. Of course, none of this comes cheap and eating out can get pretty pricey which is why, before heading off, I take a course of appetite suppressants.

Drink

Rice wine is commonly served at Phaic Tanese restaurants and can be quite enjoyable provided you don't suffer from hypertension, kidney disease or a fear of spontaneous **self-combustion**. One slightly less volatile option is *tuak*, a locally brewed beer made from the juice of **palm flowers**. It takes about three weeks to ferment and almost a year to completely leave your system. Local (grape) wine is also available but the prices are prohibitive, as is the taste. Remember, too, that the Phaic Tanese prefer their wines on the sweet side and upon ordering a bottle of **chardonnay** it is not unusual to be asked 'one lump or two?'.

Traveller's Tip

Confused by the vast array of dishes on a Phaic Tanese menu? Many diners enjoy having the chef choose for them. The chef does too as this often gives him an opportunity to get rid of last weeks' pickled catfish.

Jonathan Writes... *For the Luxury Traveller*

Phaic Tanese wine certainly has a long way to go and even their more expensive *grandes cuvées* could benefit from cellaring – preferably in a sealed concrete bunker. My advice is to stick with the local rice wine, which is similar to sake except for its colour (blue) and taste which could best be described as 'full-bodied, with a subtle hint of ethanol'. The alternative is to just drink water but personally I haven't done this since 1965.

KEEPING IT UP...

There's no denying that Phaic Tanese men have a great liking for any food stuff thought to hold aphrodisiac or 'performance-enhancing' qualities. Hence, they will voraciously devour buffalo horn powder, pickled turtle flipper, snake blood, tiger penis or bird's nest soup. Strangely, the arrival of Viagra has been treated with skepticism.

A Taste of Phaic Tan...

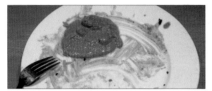

Etiquette Tip In Phaic Tanese restaurants and homes it is considered polite to leave some food on your plate. Not only is this good manners, it may give the forensic toxicologist investigating your death something to work with.

Phaic Tanese chillies rank as some of the hottest in the world, so much so that it is illegal to eat them and then belch on days of high fire danger.

Nergak (above left) is a spicy fish sauce widely added to food throughout Phaic Tan. It is made at a massive processing plant in Pattaponga (above right), one of the biggest factories in Asia, said to be the only man-made structure that can be smelt from the moon.

Typical spices used in Phaic Tanese cuisine include (from bottom left) turmeric, cummin, chilli and gunpowder.

Pu Wiph is a tuberous fruit said to combine the smell of blue cheese with the texture of straw matting. As for its taste, no one has ever been game to try it.

For a chance to sample authentic Phaic Tanese food, go no further than a traditional open-air street stall or sahlmonellah.

Kitchen staff at some of Phaic Tan's top restaurants can spend up to four days just to prepare a single dim-sim.

Snake wine is often served with its own tourniquet.

Folk Music

Phaic Tanese folk music (*Twing-Twang*) employs string and bamboo instruments along with **metal cymbals**, and has for centuries been used in folk ceremonies, religious festivals and to extract confessions from **political prisoners**. The most commonly heard instrument is the *klangpaan* (left), a saucer-shaped pewter bell generally beaten with a mallet, as is the player should he stray too far

off the beat. Few words can describe the captivating, frenetic, thunderous, **rhythmic sounds** produced by a *klangpaan*. Certainly not 'melodic' or 'soothing'. Imagine a monkey wrench striking a radiator, and then imagine that sound lasting for several hours. Originally designed as a **solo instrument**, the *klangpaan* is often accompanied by the sound of people rapidly moving away. Interestingly, there is no written music for the

klangpaan, its repertoire having been passed down, like herpes, through oral transmission.

In 1973, Khuan Phriyah (1952–81), an innovative local musician (left), announced he had invented an electrified klangpaan *that could significantly amplify the instrument's sound. He was immediately arrested and the plans destroyed.*

During the 60s many Phaic Tanese folk groups were forced to practise in secret. This was not due to government policy, it was a result of their neighbours complaining.

These days the *klangpaan* is generally combined with other traditional Phaic Tanese instruments such as the *pharta*, a sort of woodwind flute, as well as a **banjo-like device** known as a *bungstrum*. Traditionally the *bungstrum* consists of seven strings, two of which are plucked while the remaining five are used to hold the instrument together. Animal skin drums, gongs wheel rims and **wok lids** are also used extensively.

Royal Orchestra

The best way to hear these instruments is from a distance. You might consider attending a concert given by the Phaic Tanese Royal Orchestra who performs regularly throughout the country. Typically, this orchestra is made up of 12 musicians. What the other 27 people are doing on stage remains a **mystery**. Don't be put off by initial impressions – the music can at first sound a little jarring to western ears, but after a while a certain **numbness** sets in.

Phaic Tanese music is built round a **seven note octave** (the note D being considered unlucky) with no sharps, flats or rests. The concept of **pianissimo** has only recently been de-criminalized.

A local Phaic Tanese musician demonstrates a traditional kwawalom *(ventolin inhaler).*

The pharta *(above) produces a low drone that has been likened to the sound of a buffalo giving birth.*

Orchestral Order

Interestingly, Phaic Tanese conductors are the only orchestral leaders in the world not to use a baton, preferring instead a truncheon or short whip.

Phaic Tanese Pop

Popular music in Phaic Tan is generally considered to have begun with legendary vocalist Kewan Tapsikan who managed to combine **traditional Buddhist** chants with a folk rock groove. Tapsikan pretty much dominated the local charts throughout the 70s and was so popular that he was given a royally sponsored **cremation** when he died in 1984 and again in 1986 when a psychic predicted his spirit was attempting a comeback.

Classic Rock

Rock 'n' roll became a potent force during the **student uprisings** of the 1980s when Bumpattabumpah-based heavy metal outfit Raataataat galvanized the younger generation with their provocative, anti-government lyrics. So powerful was their message that the authorities attempted to stop the band recording but Raataataat refused to be silenced. Things reached a head in 1988 when they played at an **outdoor protest rally**, whipping the crowd into a frenzy with their defiant anthem 'Stand and Fight'. By the time police raided the event every member of Raataataat had fled to the hills but several thousand of their fans were arrested.

Heavy metal rockers Raataataat, taken shortly before their drummer was arrested for not wearing a tie.

COVER NOTE

In Phaic Tan not only are foreign films dubbed, so too are most western pop songs, with the biggest hits in the world all becoming cover versions, re-voiced by local performers. Since crooning tends to be the vocal style of choice in Phaic Tan, even the heaviest of international rock 'n' roll bands have a distinct 'love ballad' feel.

One of Phaic Tan's most popular Captain and Tenille tribute bands pluck out a tune.

Modern Sounds

During the 90s Phaic Tan's pop music scene was pretty much made up of **boy bands** such as Hwu2 and Mhah Mhai, who produced highly commercialized, western-sounding albums of little real note. The lead singer of Hwu2, Kee Throhng, announced he was going solo in 1995, citing the fact that the rest of the band was heading in a different direction (Kuala Lumpur).

Since then Kee has produced a string of hits and become, arguably, Phaic Tan's first real 'pop star'. With a musical style best described as '**country and eastern**', Throhng's first single 'Love Girl' was a chart smash and he went on to sweep the field at the MTV Asia Awards, picking up numerous accolades including the coveted '**Best Lip-Sync Performance**'.

His next single was a complete departure – it was in tune – and further boosted the Kee Throhng phenomena. By this stage he was recording, touring, appearing in Phaic Tan's highest rating soap opera *Hhunwan* (about two rival families of kick boxers) and working his way through puberty, an enormous load for any performer. Something had to give and in 1997 Kee attempted suicide by drinking tap water. Miraculously, he survived and went on to release a **comeback single** that many critics consider the finest offering from this dynamic young vocalist – it was almost entirely an **instrumental**.

The legendary Hakul Prubon is generally regarded as Phaic Tan's 'Queen of Pop', with dozens of hits to his name.

Suttee Kharamasi

'THE HEART ALWAYS HURT'
(Music & lyrics by S. Kharamasi)

Love me, baby – love me do

My hungry sideburns
are pointing at you.

At your ebony eyes

At your ruby lips

At the deep pink upon
your cheeks

At your flaming hair
with crimson tips.

You are the darkest beauty
of all the masses

Either that, or it's my
tinted glasses.

The biggest musical name right now would have to be Suttee Kharamasi, whose hits include 'Baby It Feel So Good' and 'The Heart Always Hurt', both of which went **bamboo** within just a few days of release. Tragically, Suttee was seriously injured outside his home recently when a shrine built by fans to ensure a long life collapsed on him. The teen star was rushed to hospital where he spent 30 days in a **coma** until his mother walked in one morning and put on his latest CD. According to eyewitnesses, Suttee suddenly woke up, after a patient in the next bed began screaming loudly, and miraculously managed to stand. He then punched his mother. Suttee was released from hospital a week later and, despite having suffered **severe brain damage**, it does not appear to have affected his song writing ability.

Of course, rock 'n' roll is all about rebellion and even in a conservative country like Phaic Tan musical stars continue to shock. At the recent Tehkas (Phaic Tan's equivalent of the Grammies) there was near outrage when two female presenters provocatively leant over to each other and shook hands.

Dance

Traditional Phaic Tanese dances can be grouped into **three broad categories**: instructive or didactic dances which are dramas with a moral; dances that purify and protect a place from demonic spirits; and the ***Macarena***.

The National Academy of Fine Arts in Bumpattabumpah is the place students go to learn **traditional dance**. Here they practise up to eight hours per week, seven days a month, learning the many subtle movements and gestures that make up a **complicated routine**.

The Academy stages regular concerts and visitors lucky enough to be in the audience are often struck by the way every movement is formed in **perfect harmony**, the emphasis being on the eyes, head and elbows. The legs are rarely moved, except at the end of a performance when the dancers rush around collecting tips. Traditional dancers will often wear **elaborate gold masks** that add a touch of drama to the performance as well as protect their face from projectiles thrown by **disgruntled audience members**.

FOLK DANCE

Less formal is the Ihamvoc, Phaic Tan's national folk dance in which participants rotate in concentric circles, getting closer and closer until a fight breaks out.

Sven Writes...
For the Budget Traveller

Catching a cultural performance overseas can be fascinating but a little pricey. By waiting outside a concert hall or theatre and asking departing audience members to describe the show to you, it's possible to share the magic without blowing big bucks on tickets.

(Left) Students at the National Academy of Fine Arts perform a scene from the traditional Dance of the Golden Beekeepers.

Literature

Phaic Tanese literature has existed for centuries in the form of fairy tales, proverbs, **simple poems** and fridge magnets. Poetry is particularly valued and some literary historians believe that the first limerick ever written originated in Phaic Tan sometime during the 7th century. Unfortunately only fragments of this work still exist, including the opening line:

Hua oax pha coa dan ni san
('There was a young girl from Nahntukkhet...')

Every school child in Phaic Tan is taught to recite at least a few lines from the great **epic poem** the *Mhahamaybrahama* that tells the story of a young man pondering the question 'which has greater beauty – the banzan tree or the lotus flower?' The fact the author takes over 1400 verses to reach the conclusion that they're both 'splendid' is considered a **masterpiece of poetic procrastination**.

ALL THE WORLD'S A STAGE!
Phaic Tan has been active in attracting visits from international artists and shows. Just last year they came very close to securing Barbra Streisand, the tour only being cancelled when promoters could not guarantee a clause in her rider demanding no tarantulas back stage. Of course, the country's standing as a showbiz tour destination took a major blow in 2003 when Disney's *Beauty and the Beast on Ice* tour had to be tragically cut short after the stadium's refrigerated stage floor broke down causing three cast members to nearly drown.

Modern Phaic Tanese theatre does away with props, elaborate costumes and – in most cases – audiences.

Despite constant threat of legal action, Phaic Tanese newspapers continue to publish their own Manga-inspired version of **Peanuts**.

The Ranayayan

This famous allegory is an essential part of Phaic Tan's cultural heritage, featuring in everything from song, dance, art and sculpture to a **long-running television soap opera**. Its central character is Ranyan, a violent, blood-thirsty tyrant who betrays and brutally kills every member of his family. He is the hero of the story. *The Ranayayan* has **many variations** but its central plot is as follows:

rince Ranyan is travelling to market one morning when he comes across a young peasant girl Siva and is struck by her beauty. Siva is then struck by his club and dragged off into the forest. But before Ranyan can have his way with her the figure of Deyar the Monkey King appears, disguised as a bird who distracts Ranyan long enough for Siva to escape by disguising herself as Lahksma, the goddess of middle distance running. Saddened by his loss, Ranyan sits by a river where he catches sight of Tekkan, an oracle god, disguised as himself, who tells him to find his one true love. Ranyan then embarks on an odyssey of seduction, courting all the women in the land, never finding true love but enjoying himself immensely along the way. By the time Ranyan finally catches up with Siva (typically a period of seven years) she is disguised as a humble wood-cutter. In a fit of rage Ranyan chops the wood-cutter into hundreds of pieces at which point her pendant, disguised as a bracelet, falls at his feet revealing he has just dismembered the only woman he ever truly loved.

Ranayayan – Principal Characters

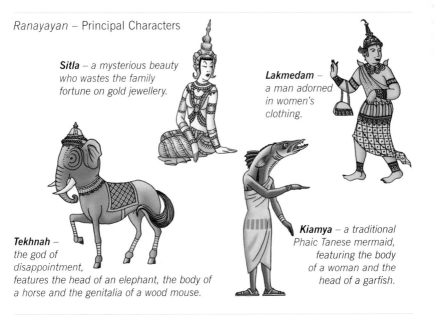

Sitla – *a mysterious beauty who wastes the family fortune on gold jewellery.*

Lakmedam – *a man adorned in women's clothing.*

Tekhnah – *the god of disappointment, features the head of an elephant, the body of a horse and the genitalia of a wood mouse.*

Kiamya – *a traditional Phaic Tanese mermaid, featuring the body of a woman and the head of a garfish.*

Sport
Kick Boxing

To say that the Phaic Tanese love their kick boxing would be an understatement and boys as young as five are regularly taken away to **national training camps** where they are taught to kick and punch for hours on end. After many years a successful few go on to become 'Grand Masters', while those who fail return home to work as **insurance brokers**.

Many visitors to Phaic Tan are keen to witness a kick boxing match and there are events held just about every night of the week. **Ticket prices** vary depending on where you sit – expect to pay extra for anywhere close enough to be **showered in blood**.

Bouts are accompanied by wild music and wild betting as fans work themselves into a frenzy. Contestants wear **baggy trunks** (in which extra weapons may often be concealed) as well as gloves. Feet are bare (women may wear heels) and most fighters also wear **sacred headbands** into the ring for good luck. These are removed before the match and often used later by losing contestants to strangle their trainer.

GOING FOR GOLD...
Desperate for their sport to be given Olympic accreditation, a group of officials from the Phaic Tanese Kick Boxing Federation (P.H.K.W.F.) recently travelled to Lausanne to argue their case. Unfortunately the cause was not helped when one over-enthusiastic member of the delegation ended his power point presentation by smashing the overhead projector with a spinning side-kick.

Phaic Tanese kick-boxing, or Hi Kik Wak, is similar to the Thai version except that competitors may, in addition to kicking and punching, also use broken bottles.

BE WARNED
In rural areas fights can get pretty brutal with bouts rarely stopped until at least one contestant is either dead or an organ donor.

KICK BOXING KING...

You don't have to travel far in Phaic Tan to hear the name **Trong Tchen**, believed by many to be the greatest kick boxer in the history of the sport.

Born in the country's south in 1962, Tchen was quite short-sighted and one day on his way to school a group of local youths taunted the young boy about his glasses. The story goes that the following day Tchen returned and single-handedly exacted his revenge. Unfortunately, due to his **short sightedness** he got the wrong group and was subsequently charged with assaulting a cub scout pack.

Struck by their son's fanatic devotion to fitness and obvious violent streak, his parents pushed him into competitive ballroom dancing but the young Tchen clearly preferred martial arts. Within months he was competing in national kick boxing tournaments and by the age of 17 had attained *meuysan* status, meaning he was officially recognized as a Grand Master, as well as being licensed to work as a professional crowd controller.

At the age of 23 Trong Tchen suffered a **serious injury** when a feng shui deflector installed on the roof of his training gym blew off and landed on his neck. A doctor summoned to treat the legendary sportsman declared he would never fight again. Tchen proved this prognosis wrong by landing a powerful blow to the medico's midriff, before returning to the ring a few weeks later.

At the height of his powers it was said that Trong Tchen could spin 360 degrees on one foot seven times per second. This awesome ability meant he only ever lost one professional bout, and that was on a technicality (dizziness).

After retiring from the ring Tchen went on to a **successful and prolific film career** (see over) and his 1987 master-work *Instep of Fear* remains the highest grossing film in Phaic Tanese history. He died in 1993 after an **ill-fated comeback** attempt involving an exhibition match between martial arts champions and wild animals (the bear won on a split points decision). Trong Tchen is buried in the Bumpattabumpah cemetary and a large shrine there still attracts hundreds of fans every year who come to pay their respects by attempting to crack the **marble headstone** with a single kick.

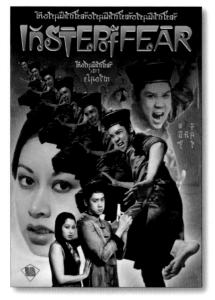

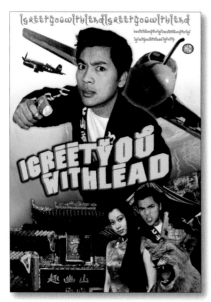

Kick boxing champion Trong Tchen went on to become one of Phaic Tan's most popular film stars, appearing in over 40 titles. Amongst his classic works are (clockwise from top left) the cult classic Instep of Fear, *the romantic comedy* Death Wish for Two, *the spy thriller* I Greet You with Lead *and the critically ignored* Hamlet.

Cock Fighting

Despite various attempts to ban it, cock fighting remains a hugely **popular sport** in Phaic Tan with thousands of matches held every day throughout the country.

COCK CRAZY

Residents of Phaic Tan's northern provinces have combined two great sporting passions by teaching their roosters to kick box. So popular have these events become that in the mid-90s the WWF began televising bouts. Recently an estimated TV audience of 3.8 million tuned into a special pay-per-view event *Cockamania III*. Other broadcasts include *Rage in a Cage*, *Quack Down!* and *Smack-A-Doodle-Doo*.

Fights are generally 'to the death' with the loser ending up as chicken nuggets. Champion cocks are highly prized for their **ferocity and aggression** and will often fight for up to 10 years after which time they are 'retired' and sold as **children's pets**. Recently Phaic Tan was chosen as host nation for the next Southeast Asian Cock Fighting Championships 'Peckfest 2008'.

Asian Octathlon

Introduced by Phaic Tan at the recent Southeast Asian Games this gruelling event involves **eight separate disciplines**: table tennis, badminton, hacky sack, kick boxing, synchronized ten pin bowling, long-tail boat racing, mah jong and yo-yo tricks.

The Phaic Tanese synchronized ten-pin bowling team go through their paces.

Traditional Martial Arts

The ancient art of *kaitooh* is practised throughout Phaic Tan. This **tradition** focuses heavily on hand-held weapons, including the *pon* (sword), *sep* (quarter-staff), *boun* (a ceremonial shield), *drak* (a pair of swords held in both hands) and *akun* (a long handled club). The two combatants face off in a **marked ring**, circling each other until one collapses under the weight of his or her weaponry.

Top Spinning

Tih Di, or top spinning, is a sport practised seriously by adults in Phaic tan. The **wooden tops**, made from teak, can weigh up to 5kg and spin for as long as two hours. Competitions usually involve two tops being made to spin inside a **marked circle**. The losing player is the first person to fall asleep.

Other sports

In many villages a primitive version of football is played in which a **woven rattan ball** or small pet is kicked around. Basketball is also popular although given that the average height in Phaic Tan remains at the lower end of the spectrum it is legal to slam dunk with the aid of a **stepladder**.

Karaoke

The people of Phaic Tan are absolutely passionate about karaoke – even though not technically a sport – and regularly compete against each other for **large cash prizes**. So obsessive can they be that when the capital's largest karaoke bar caught fire in 1998, hundreds were killed as they insisted on staying behind and singing the theme from *Towering Inferno*.

SPORTING SUPERSTAR

Despite being a non-contact sport, table tennis is well loved by the Phaic Tanese and many remember fondly the exploits of their country's most gifted exponent, the legendary Tommy 'Tuk Tuk' Pyhong (1965–93). His signature shot was known as the King Cobra in which he would jump, spin and – in a flash of stunning contortion – smash the ball. Tommy's action was so fast it was said he could play himself – and lose. His career was tragically cut short at the '93 Regional Championships when, after a particularly hard fought victory, he attempted to jump the net and was crushed by the collapsing table.

Traveller's Tip

When playing Phaic Tanese Scrabble (*Xienq Quxong*) remember that X and Q are worth only two points.

Film & TV

A number of major Hollywood films have used Phaic Tan as a setting although few have had much in the way of box office success. *Love Me, Love My Fist* was to be the first foray into **romantic comedy** for Chuck Norris but filming had to be cancelled due to **heavy monsoonal rains** in the country's west, while *Out of Hope*, a chilling sci-fi fantasy about the world being reduced to a squalid, post-nuclear slum was filmed entirely in the outer suburbs of Bumpattabumpah. The Leonardo DiCaprio epic *The Beach* was very nearly shot in Phaic Tan, its producers only pulling out after two location scouts were kidnapped and held to ransom during a pre-production recce.

If you plan on seeing a film in Phaic Tan, remember that the advertised start time actually refers to when the national anthem will be played. This is generally followed by a series of **short educational films** with titles such as *King Tralanhng – A Monarch for All Seasons* and then half an hour of ads for tobacco products after which time the film – or what's left of it after **local censors** have removed any scenes deemed offensive or unlucky – will commence.

Phaic Tanese cinema artists are often quite 'liberal' in their interpretation of Hollywood stars. Above is a poster depicting Tom Cruise and Whoopee Goldberg.

There are three television channels in Phaic Tan. K-TV is devoted entirely to kick boxing. G-TV is a government station on which 'journalists' deliver thinly disguised propaganda – it is largely based on America's Fox News channel. The third, PT-TV, is worth watching for a useful insight into local culture.

PT/TV

06:00am	**Yoga** Wake and stretch to a new day with Swami Bhendit.
07:00am	**Morning news** A man with glasses and a woman with a bob speak very fast.
08:00am	**Hau Da Phuk?** Children's science show hosted by Professor Hoo Wen Wai.
09:00am	**Epaulette Street** Popular soap opera about a group of military leaders who live on the same street. General Sambuck is ridiculed for never having led a coup.
11:00am	**Ground Force** Lifestyles series. Today the team have 24 hours to de-mine a backyard before the owners return home.
12:00pm	**Days of Your Lives** Buddhist drama.
03:30pm	**Love Resort** Soap opera set in a Pattaponga high-rise hotel. Today, the owner's daughter falls for the unconventional concierge.
05:00pm	**People's Court Martial** Real life cases, presided over by Judge Judo.
06:00pm	**Parliament** Recorded highlights of today's brawls.
07:30pm	**Who Wants To Be a Millionaire?** One of the few versions where a contestant may choose to either phone a friend or consult a psychic.
08:30pm	**Big Buddha** 12 novice monks are locked in a temple for 16 weeks with cameras catching their every move.
10:30pm	**Queen's message** (Available in wide-screen)
12:00am	**Closure** Singing of the national anthem followed by the reaffirmation of isolationism.

Geography

Phaic Tan has a varied and lush topography with tropical forests, **craggy mountains**, sweeping plains, two river deltas and an extensive coastline, much of it lined by water. The country also claims numerous islands off its coast, including Phra Salahng, Na Chok and – somewhat controversially – Borneo.

The north and south of Phaic Tan are virtually severed by a line of **volcanoes**, the biggest being the active, smoke-belching Gunsa Wah ('God's bottom'). This volcano last erupted in 1988, filling the air with thick smoke and ash for miles around. At the time no one actually noticed, assuming it was simply a local **logging contractor** carrying out a routine 'slash and burn' operation.

MM **BUMPATTABUMPAH ANNUAL RAINFALL**

500_
400_
300_
200_
100_
0
   J F M A M J J A S O N D

*Clearly June or July – the Dry Season – is **the** time to travel to Phaic Tan.*

CLIMATE CHANGE
Core samples have revealed that Phaic Tan has experienced profound periods of humidity through the last fifty thousand years, so much so that the Iron Age was actually followed by a Rust Age. During this period the country's rainforests retreated and over 70% of Phaic Tan was covered in mildew.

Climate

Phaic Tan's climate is ruled by monsoons and in the south there are **two distinct seasons**; a short, hot wet season (*pasaan*) and a longer, hot, even wetter season (*pannaaang*). The northeast of the country remains dry year round, perhaps explaining why **rice farmers** living there consistently struggle to survive. Being so close to the equator, Phaic Tan is extremely hot and humid year round. There was a US$3 billion **government-backed initiative** to air-condition the entire country some years back but it was scrapped after the arrival of a US$30 billion **electricity bill**.

Phaic Tan is officially hit by more cyclones, tornadoes, hurricanes and typhoons than any other country in the world. Having already gone through the Baby Names book twice, local meteorologists are now numbering **major storm events**. For example, last year the west coast was battered by Cyclone Sally the Fourth.

(Below) The north east of Phaic Tan is so humid that the mountains overlooking the Donkekong flood plains are suffering from rising damp. Geologists have dubbed this condition as 'tinea of the foothills'.

Phaic Tan has the highest rate of air conditioners per head of population in the world. A resident on the top floor of this Bumpattabumpah apartment block was actually admitted to hospital with frostbite.

KEEPING COOL!

If you think Phaic Tan's heat and humidity are hard to take now, spare a thought for those who lived here back before the arrival of electric cooling. In those days rooms were kept ventilated with a ceiling fan pulled by a young servant boy (*mataak*) who customarily sat outside. With the coming of electricity in the 1920s this system was modified; the young servant boy still sat outside pulling the fan but he had a wire cable attached to one toe and was given a jolt if he slowed down.

Economy

Not a country blessed with an abundance of **natural resources** (tin and aluminium are still considered semiprecious metals), Phaic Tan relies heavily on its agricultural sector.

The principal commercial crop is rubber with an estimated 70,000ha of **plantations** across the country. However, Phaic Tanese rubber is considered to be of poor quality, as it doesn't stretch or bend and has a tendency to dissolve when exposed to moisture. (It does, however, make excellent **squash balls** which has proved a saviour of the industry.)

Other crops include bananas, pineapples, sugarcane, maize and rice. In the north of the country many **hill-tribe farmers** still cultivate opium poppies although in recent years the Government has been encouraging them to take up more appropriate crops, such as **marijuana**.

PHAIC TAN'S TOP 5 EXPORTS*

1 MSG

2 Beaded Car Seat Covers

3 Spring Roll Wrappers

4 Crab sticks

5 Dengue Fever

*Souce: OECD 2003–2004

HEALTH FACT

In recent years Phaic Tan has made great advances in reducing its rate of infant and maternal mortality but sadly many thousand Phaic Tanese fathers still die during childbirth, the result of celebrating with unregulated fireworks displays.

Military Might

The Phaic Tanese army was estimated at 130,000; however, it has recently been discovered that many of these are '**ghost soldiers**' for whom Commander in Chief General Midaak has been claiming salaries. Actual troop numbers in the five **infantry divisions** are currently put at 12.

Securing **foreign investment** has been difficult although in 2002 the Phaic Tan economy received a welcome US$20 million injection after an aircraft belonging to a Chicago bank was accidentally shot down by government troops over Hoipac.

In the Phaic Tanese military rank is indicated by the size of one's helmet. This man is a junior officer.

LIQUID BROWN

Recent hopes of a major crude oil discovery in the southern city of Miar Hop were dashed after test results revealed the exploration team had accidentally tapped into the town's main sewer.

While many northern Phaic Tanese farmers insist they are merely growing herbal tea, the presence of electrified wire fencing, spotlights, dogs and armed labourers often makes this claim a little hard to take seriously.

(Left) Phaic Tan is also a major contributor to the international spice trade, supplying over 70% of the world's capsicum spray.

Ecology & the Environment

With an enormous population packed into a relatively small country, there is understandably **significant pressure** on Phaic Tan's ecosystems. Perhaps the worst affected areas are the forests where wide scale **logging operations** have led to entire mountains washing away. As a result, Phaic Tan boasts some of the most heavily silted rivers in Southeast Asia. In the Nahkthong Delta, for example, scientists estimate there is actually more soil than water, and many fish living here have been found to suffer from **gravel rash**.

Recent attempts to convert all motor vehicles to LPG gas have met with limited success.

The Forests

Phaic Tan is working hard to stem the flow of **illegally harvested timber** leaving the country and as of 2003 departing visitors have been permitted to take no more than two logs each. In a bid to protect its remaining forests the government has established **numerous reserves** in which timber harvesting is banned. To make absolutely sure it doesn't happen, all trees have been removed from these reserves.

TREE HUGGING

In the face of mounting international criticism of their logging policies the Phaic Tanese Government insists that 60% virgin forest cover still remains, although it should be borne in mind that their official definition of 'rainforest' includes scrubland, rice paddies, golf courses, artificial tennis courts and balconies with one or more hanging basket.

Strict new environmental laws insist all coastal sewage outlets must be at least 20m from the water.

The Oceans

Off-shore, things are little better, with pollution and poaching both taking their toll. **Heavy metal** contamination of the waters off eastern Phaic Tan has been so bad that many of the fish there are caught with **magnets**.

Deep sea species are also vulnerable to long-line fishing as well as a new technique called **very long-line fishing**, in which the fleets are based in Japan.

The Phaic Tanese Government has threatened to get tough on illegal fishing and recently purchased a 'patrol boat' for its **marine officers** but so far the vessel's effectiveness has been limited by the time-consuming process of inflating it every time a pursuit is required. Their first arrest was actually a member of their own crew found illegally trolling en route to an interception.

Coral Care

Another ecological step forward has been the passage of laws to phase out the practice of coral dynamiting by coastal developers. **Coral dynamiting** will, however, remain legal as a recreational pursuit.

Due to a lack of environmental controls, the sand along much of Phaic Tan's coast is now a curious mix of silica (3%), quartz (7%) and clay (90%). This hasn't stopped tourism though, and beaches such as Qog Miah (above) are proudly promoted as the place 'where Surf meets Sludge'.

Flora

Years of warfare and civil unrest have left their mark on Phaic Tan and until recently its **floral emblem** was defined as 'any shrub that could provide cover during an ambush'. These days the **official flower** is of course the wilting orchid (left), known officially as *Suahm* in honour of Her Majesty the Queen with whom it is said to share many qualities, such as beauty, grace and difficulties retaining moisture. Other indigenous species include the Flowering Bok Choy (also known as Bok Chulip) and the Brocconvillea.

Much of Phaic Tan is covered in **dense jungle** except in the slightly drier north eastern regions where rainforest gives way to **drizzle forest**. Here you'll find a bewildering variety of exotic plants, including the massive sahthien pine, renowned as one of the few trees in the world to shed not just leaves but entire branches.

SITUATIONS VACANT
Despite government attempts to stop them, armed poachers still run unchecked, with much of the illicit trade controlled by organized Chinese gangs. Forestry rangers are paid very little (although they are allowed to keep any bullets fired into them) and struggle to protect often vast areas of forest. A recent scheme to boost numbers has involved prisoners on death row being offered a reprieve from the firing squad if they agree to work for six months as a forest ranger. At the time of writing no one had accepted the offer.

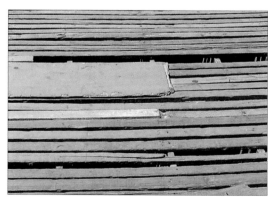

CHEAP TEAK
Phaic Tanese teak is not so highly sought after due to its extremely poor quality. The wood is also coarse grained, resists sanding and is almost invariably infested with termites. Because of this, local teak is mainly used as firewood or to build passenger ferries.

Many Phaic Tanese trees are so brittle they require extensive artificial support if they are to grow beyond the size of a small shrub.

The sathien pine, one of the few trees in the world to shed entire branches.

WOODS WARRIOR

The fact that many of Phaic Tan's more exotic rainforest plant species survive at all is largely thanks to one woman, Triong Kapthala (1947–98). Known as the 'Woods Warrior', Kapthala was a passionate botanist who actually had several types of fungus named after her. But it was Phaic Tan's precious hardwood trees that she most fought to protect and during the 1980s this passionate environmentalist led numerous campaigns against unscrupulous logging contractors. Ironically, Triong Kapthala was killed in 1998 when the branch of a large rainforest tree fell on her. The fact she was sleeping in her city apartment at the time was dismissed as a coincidence by authorities.

Fauna

As with its plant life, Phaic Tan's **bloody past** has certainly taken its toll on its animal inhabitants, with dozens of species all but wiped out in armed conflict. Some have managed to survive by adapting, such as the wild *Buaktong* goats of the east which – after decades of **border skirmishes** – have actually developed bullet-proof hides. Sadly, though, many creatures are under threat of extinction, in particular monkeys, elephants, wild cattle and environmental activists. **Breeding programs** currently exist for several endangered species unique to Phaic Tan, such as the magnificent spotless leopard, the rarely sighted buck-toothed tiger and the myopic owl, a bird so short-sighted it has been known to swoop on ceramic cats.

Long thought to be extinct, small herds of the Klow Gyar Ox have recently been discovered in eastern Phaic Tan. Excited local naturalists describe them as looking a little like a Brahman bull and tasting a little like pork.

Phaic Tan is home to one of the world's highest number of near-extinct species. Amongst those creatures not sighted in decades are:

> **The Stuttering Parrot**

> **The Thinning Lion** – one of the few felines ever recorded whose mane requires a comb-over.

> **The Bow-legged Asian Elephant**

> **The Lanky Pelican** (*Pelicanus aneorexicus*)

> **The Hunch-backed Rhino**

> **The Long-haired Turtle**

Phaic Tan boasts some unusual fish, including a local species of carp, believed to be the boniest fish known to man. Their hardy build can see them live for 25 years, or 50 if anti-arthritics are added to their food. Phaic Tan's rivers also play home to the cholu, the only piranha in the world to suffer from an overbite.

(Opposite top) The endangered Phaic Tanese elephant is so used to being hunted that in the wild many have developed the ability to shed their horns at the slightest sound of a human approaching.

(Opposite below) As the rainforests of Phaic Tan recede, so too have the hairlines of its largest tree-dweller, the Balding Ape. A government-sponsored plan to aerial spray their habitats with Rogaine is currently being considered.

Architecture

In the field of sculpture and architecture the Phaic Tanese rarely displayed the virtuosity or creativity of many of their neighbours. A lack of **durable building materials**, coupled with the people's fundamental inability to draw straight lines, impeded major advances in the construction field.

But Phaic Tan certainly does have its share of **man-made treasures**, none more famous than the capital Bumpattabumpah's magnificent Opera House. Completed in 1910, this grand edifice is tiered like a **massive rice paddy**, a theme carried through to the auditorium's interior design where the orchestra pit is actually under water for much of the year and the conductor sits on a **lifeguard's chair**. Further afield, the country is dotted with historic temples, shrines, palaces and **mobile small arms factories**, many of which are open to the public. As for private dwellings, you'll notice that most houses in Phaic Tan are built on stilts which not only provides **ventilation**, it prevents elderly relatives from moving in.

Whether old or new, all Phaic Tanese houses are constructed in the same basic way – without building approval.

The magnificent gilded gate of Phrayamak was built in 1982 to celebrate a visit by the Royal Family. Sadly, the gate was officially declared closed when it was realised that Her Majesty Queen Luprang could not actually fit through.

Shopping

Phaic Tanese shopping centres offer a **huge range** of silk, fashion, shoes, jewellery and handicrafts. The only down-side is that these goods are generally of **poor quality** and made in Taiwan.

For a more 'authentic' experience, visit one of the many teeming **street bazaars** you'll find throughout the country. These are a wonderful way to pick up bargains and even the most half-hearted shopper will come away with something, whether it's silk clothing, jewellery or simply an **upper respiratory infection**.

Of course, for the ultimate in retail therapy you can't go past one of Phaic Tan's new **mega malls**, such as the King Tralanhng centre in Bumpattabumpah. A massive building – so large it has three separate time zones – the Tralanhng centre also happens to boast the largest **ceiling fan** in the world, made from the blades of a de-commissioned Black Hawk helicopter.

Colourful chemical dyes used widely in children's breakfast cereals.

Phaic Tan's markets are a great place to shop for children's clothing.

Fabrics

Phaic Tanese silk is considered some of the finest in the world, despite its **coarse weave** and tendency to tear when folded. It is used widely throughout the country in everything from ceremonial wedding dresses to firing squad blindfolds and disposable kitchen wipes.

A shopkeeper waits for customers outside a Phaic Tanese second-hand garbage stall.

While customer satisfaction levels may vary, Phaic Tanese stores boast some of the world's happiest mannequins.

Tina Writes...
For the Cautious Traveller

When trying on clothes in overseas shops, refuse offers to use their changing room. The scourge of hidden cameras has arrived even here and next thing you're appearing on some grubby internet site in your underwear. Stop these perverts in their tracks by insisting on getting changed in the middle of the shop.

Clothing

An **extraordinary range** of fashion is available in Phaic Tan and shoppers who buy shirts and suits here are often surprised, not just by the prices, but by the way the sleeves tend to fall off without warning.

Jewellery

Diamonds and precious stones are sold throughout Phaic Tan but it is gold that people most often come here for. There are **gold markets** throughout the larger cities and it's easy to tell the good ones, as they've usually just been robbed.

Hill-tribe Crafts

These include ceramic bowls and opium smoking accessories as well as the popular *luah mi*, a type of **intricately woven basket** made from a hardy grass found in northern Phaic Tan. Baskets of this style make an excellent gift, usually to **quarantine officers** at your home airport as they carry wood borer and are rarely allowed in.

The women of Pha Phlung are skilled at turning fruit and vegetables into colourful hats.

Lacquerware

The tradition of lacquerware was begun in the 11th century by eastern villagers to provide a light, flexible, waterproof cover for their cattle. It was later applied to furniture, bowls, trays, plates, boxes and – in more recent times – artificial limbs. The actual process is incredibly time-consuming and, using **traditional methods**, it can take up to six months to produce a single soup bowl which, in many cases, will be highly porous.

Toys

Shops and street stalls in Phaic Tan are a good place to buy **children's toys** that have been banned in other countries as dangerous. In fact, the Kuaph Pahn department store in Bumpattabumpah has an entire floor devoted to **choking hazards**.

Simple pleasures!
A happy Phaic Tanese
child plays with a tyre
stolen from a tourist's car.

LET'S MAKE A DEAL Bargaining, haggling, call it what you will, Phaic Tanese love the ritual of negotiating a price and tend to make an art form of it. In many cities it's not unusual to see the victim of a road accident arguing with paramedics over the quoted cost of hospital transportation. When haggling with a shopkeeper don't be put off by angry looks and throat-slitting gestures – these are all part of the theatre – although should he produce a knife or small handgun it might be worth edging towards the door. The rules of haggling are simple. Ask how much an item costs – whatever the shopkeeper says, offer them 50%. The shopkeeper will look shocked and may even faint or attempt self-immolation. Keep smiling and wait for their next offer. Good luck!

Philippe Writes...

I laugh at western tourists who get a small discount after five minutes of to-ing and fro-ing, then leave thinking they've 'haggled'. I once rented a room opposite an antique shop in Sloh Phan for a month just so I could get an extra 5% off a jade umbrella handle. And I succeeded.

Traveller's Tip

When planning a shopping trip to Phaic Tan, pack a spare empty suitcase. Your original one will probably be stolen.

Counterfeit Goods

There's no doubting it, Phaic Tan has become something of a centre for fake and pirated goods, ranging from DVDs and watches through to clothing and shoes. So successful have the **black market traders** become that there is now a new group of vendors emerging who specialize in selling counterfeit counterfeit goods.

Beware, many DVDs, for example, are made by someone standing at the back of a cinema and pointing a handi-cam at the screen. Given the Phaic Tanese film goers' tendency to get up and move around frequently during movies, your new blockbuster may contain little more than shots of someone in silhouette eating popcorn.

When it comes to clothing, even more caution is required. A close examination of those cut price 'Leevi' jeans will usually reveal **tell-tale characteristics** that they might not be authentic – three legs is often a give-away.

International fashion labels can be found throughout Phaic Tan such as Italian-based Graham Armani.

Remember, if you're buying cheap imitations, always ask for a certificate of inauthenticity.

Phaic Tan After Dark

Sadly, Phaic Tan has developed something of a reputation as the sex capital of Southeast Asia due, in part, to the large number of '**girlie bars**' and nightclubs clustered in many of its larger cities. Here, tourists can sit and enjoy a beer while watching **exotic dancers** perform on a specially elevated bar. For an additional fee these 'bar girls' will provide just about any service, with the possible exception of getting you a drink from the bar, and sexual 'treats' are clearly on the 'menu'.

Important Note *Prostitution is technically illegal in Phaic Tan and is currently the subject of an official government inquiry. This explains the large number of ministers and senior public servants often found in city brothels and bars, all attempting to gain a hands-on feel for the delicate issue.*

Massage

Traditional massage, or *Noh-Hanki-Panki*, is often associated with the sex industry but Phaic Tanese techniques in fact have very little to do with sensual pleasure. The most common form of **tactile therapy** is what's called a 'traditional' massage and is like nothing you've experienced before, unless you have recently stumbled into an electric fence. It begins with your entire body being covered from top to toe in **coconut oil.** The most unusual aspect of this procedure is that you remain fully clothed. The massage therapist then sets to work on various 'trigger' points, so-called because when pressed they trigger an enormous wave of pain. Unlike Swedish massage that seeks to relax the body through gentle kneading with the fingers and hands, Phaic Tanese therapists employ a multipronged approach using the hands, thumbs, fingers, elbows, forearms, knees and, in some cases, a **modified nail-gun**. A typical traditional massage lasts half an hour or until the client passes out.

Note If a Phaic Tanese masseuse promises a 'happy ending' this may simply mean you get to leave without having your wallet stolen.

Traveller's Tip

Be careful getting film processed in Phaic Tan's red-light districts as they will generally assume you want your faces blacked out.

Traditional Phaic Tanese masseuses will come to your hotel or home and offer services such as 'cupping' in which toxins are drawn out of the body. For a small additional fee they will also unblock your sink.

Note There is no pre-flight safety talk on Royal Fok Tok Airlines, but shortly before take-off they do screen a condensed version of Airport '75.

Traveller's Tip

Due to frequent traffic jams between the domestic and international terminal it is often quicker to fly between the two.

Sven Writes...
For the Budget Traveller

Many of the world's major airlines are based in Christian countries and if you're prepared to fly out on Christmas Day, then break your trip mid-way by stopping over in a transit lounge until Good Friday, you can save hundreds of dollars in air-fare costs.

Getting There

Most people choose to arrive in Phaic Tan by air, landing at Phlat Chat Airport. Unfortunately, many of the world's largest airlines refuse to use Phlat Chat, unhappy with the airport authority's refusal to evict the dozens of **street vendors** who have set up stalls on the edge of its runways.

The best way to get a flight in is aboard Phaic Tan's national carrier Royal Fok Tok Airlines. Named after the legendary flightless bird, Fok Tok has worked hard to lift its safety record after a minor incident in 1996 when a passenger jet overshot the end of the runway by 57 kilometres. Since then strict new rules have been passed banning **untethered livestock** in the cockpit, but Fok Tok is still battling for recognition from the international aviation community. One sticking point remains the tendency of its pilots to conserve fuel by shutting off the engines 10 minutes before landing. On the plus side, Fok Tok not only allows smoking on board, they actively encourage it, especially at night when multiple lit cigarettes make up for a distinct lack of **cabin lighting**.

If you'd rather not fly, there is an express rail service linking Phaic Tan with several neighbouring countries. Most popular is the twice-weekly **Bullet Train**, so named because it's frequently shot at during border crossings.

Despite a less than impressive safety record Royal Fok Tok Airlines was recently voted as having the 'Best Dressed Cabin Crew' in Southeast Asia.

Getting Round

Driving in Phaic Tan is not really recommended, due to the poor state of rural roads. Trips into remote village areas will almost definitely require a 4WD, preferably armour-plated, and a **police escort**.

Back in the 1980s, driving in Phaic Tan was considered risky due to the large number of highway bandits who would routinely stop motorists and extort large sums of money. These lawless rogues still exist – in fact many of them now run car rental firms – but they are no longer quite so heavily armed.

Even roads within Phaic Tan's larger towns are badly damaged from years of war and general neglect, prompting the Government to recently set up a scheme in which locals were paid a small cash reward to fill in **pot holes**. The scheme had to be quickly abandoned when it was discovered these same enterprising locals were sneaking out at night and deliberately creating new pot holes.

The **road rules** in Phaic Tan are quite straight-forward. Cars and motorbikes drive on the left, buses and trucks drive at their own discretion – at specific times of the day footpaths may be used as a transit lane. Remember to always sound your horn before overtaking, turning, pulling out, pulling in, changing lanes or stopping. It's also **obligatory** to sound your horn before sounding your horn and stiff fines apply to those who fail to do so.

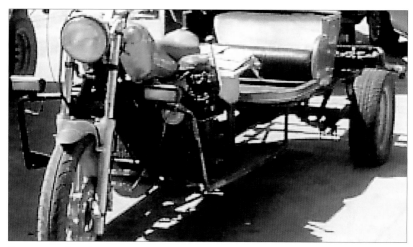

Commuters in a hurry might consider hiring a high-powered tuk tuk. A similar model recently broke the land rickshaw speed record in Utah.

(Clockwise from top) Dokar trucks are an efficient form of transport however the ox will often over-heat; a small shrub is frequently carried by drivers to protect from evil spirits and sniper attack; one of the world's first rear impact air-bags; Kayhama Square in Bumpattabumpah boasts Southeast Asia's largest single bike-rack.

Rail gauges vary throughout Phaic Tan – sometimes even on the same line.

Traveller's Tip

During a long train trip be wary of anyone arriving at your cabin and claiming to be a 'cleaner'. No such job description exists on Phaic Tan's railway system.

Bus

Phaic Tan has an efficient bus system that makes getting round the country relatively easy. However the appalling state of many roads means that it's rare to travel far without experiencing some breakdown involving either the bus or its driver. **Long-haul buses** link all the major cities and are surprisingly quick, due to the absence of any real braking mechanism. Most buses are air-conditioned and have **on-board toilet facilities**, or at very least smell as if they do.

Train

Regular train services link the north and south of the country and travellers have the choice of different speeds, including the super fast Express Sprinter class, which is used primarily for **overnight trips**, the Deluxe Plodder stopping at many smaller stations and the third-class Economy Standard, which hasn't moved since 1965. Although Phaic Tanese train travel can be **excruciatingly slow** it's a great way of meeting the locals, many of whom will be seated on your lap.

Boat

Anyone planning a visit to one of Phaic Tan's numerous off-shore islands can do so easily via the PAKT Ferry Service. **Timetables** are available throughout the country listing arrivals, departures and capsize times.

Jonathan Writes... *For the Luxury Traveller*

In my opinion, the best way to travel through a foreign country is ensconced in the plush back seat of an air-conditioned, chauffeur-driven car. One tip though – always insist on a non-English speaking driver, thus avoiding any possibility that the wretched *garçon* might attempt to strike up a conversation *en route*. Should this not be possible you may be forced to feign deafness or pretend to be sleeping for the entire trip.

Phaic Tanese public transport has very strict laws governing minimum weight limits. The bus (top) is fine but the taxi (above) is waiting for more passengers before it may legally depart.

Health & Safety

Staying healthy overseas doesn't require anything more than a few **pre-trip precautions** and general prudence. Those planning to visit Phaic Tan should discuss the trip with a doctor who may in turn refer you for **psychiatric assessment**, as well as administer a few vaccinations. The following are considered essential: cholera, yellow fever, hepatitis A, tetanus, typhoid, meningococcal, meningitis, polio, diptheria, hepatitis B, measles, mumps, rubella, varicella, haeophilus influenzae type-B, influenza and dust mite sensitivity as well as a rabies shot if you're likely to be exposed to wild animals or **street vendors**. In addition, you might require a shot for Septacemic Endyphalitis, a rare disease that strikes people who have been given too many injections.

STAYING HEALTHY

There's no definitive way of telling whether food is going to make you sick so the best thing to do is use common sense. If your instincts tell you not to eat that gelatinous chicken foot, don't eat it. Explain to your host/waiter about your 'foreign stomach' and accept a cup of tea instead. If the cup of tea contains a gelatinous chicken foot it might be worth making alternative dining arrangements.

Sven Writes...
For the Budget Traveller
The cost of vaccinations can be pretty high but most drug companies have very conservative use-by dates and if you're prepared to sign a waiver many travel clinics will prescribe cheaper medication. Find a friendly veterinarian and negotiate further discounts.

Malaria

This potentially fatal disease exists throughout the year and is spread by **mosquito bites**. Worst affected areas are low lying valleys, swamps, river flats and anywhere large amounts of stagnant water collects, such as **hotel bathrooms**. There are various forms of malaria in Phaic Tan, including a **rare strain** that is actually carried by humans and fatal to mosquitos.

Several strains of malaria unique to Phaic Tan have emerged in recent years and many of these are resistant to modern drug treatments. The most common is a particularly virulent form known as malaria type-A. Symptoms – fever, cramps, headache etc. – can be pretty severe but the good news is that they rarely last longer than a week, as death usually occurs on day five or six.

The best protection is to avoid being bitten. Mosquito nets are a good idea, preferably made of **steel mesh** and electrified. Another excellent technique is to only go out wearing long pants, a long-sleeved shirt, light cotton gloves and a head net.*

Rabies

Stray dogs can be a problem in some Phaic Tanese cities. In these areas a walking stick or umbrella provides a useful **deterrent**. They also work well on hawkers. If bitten by a dog or other suspect animal, wash the wound immediately with soap and antiseptic solution, apply a heavy **pressure bandage** and then have the limb amputated.

Sunstroke

Over-exposure to heat in a tropical country like Phaic Tan can be very dangerous. If you start feeling weak, fatigued, dizzy or disoriented, get out of the sun immediately and go to a cool, shady place, such as Norway.

Heatstroke

This is a serious, occasionally fatal condition that occurs when the body's heat-regulating mechanism breaks down. Symptoms include **severe headaches** and a lack of coordination accompanied by the sufferer becoming confused and aggressive. At this point you may be mistaken for a taxi driver. **Hospitalization** is essential.

Drinking Water

Perhaps the number one cause of health problems for travellers, contaminated water can cause a host of **unpleasant side effects**. The best advice is to only drink bottled water although care should be taken to avoid **counterfeit brands**. Typographic errors on the label are an obvious give-away here. Evian assure us they do not market a product bearing the phrase 'Natural Sprink Water, bottled at the sauce'.

* Not only will this protect against getting malaria, women are very unlikely to get pregnant.

Traveller's Tip

Phaic Tanese pharmacies carry no panadol, paracetamol or penicillin, in fact, nothing beginning with 'p' as it is considered unlucky in medicine. You can, however, ask for 'ain-killers'.

Tina Writes...
For the Cautious Traveller

Why have a trip spoilt by contaminated water when it's so easy to avoid? Whenever I'm invited out to a new overseas restaurant I take a small portable gas stove and boil every drink as it arrives, even beer. If I'm still not convinced of the beverage's purity I dose it with iodine before running the contents through a hand operated filter. Simple.

Bronze monument dedicated to Randy Taylor, the only westerner to be admitted to Bumpattabumpah Hospital with constipation.

Doctors & Hospitals

If you do get sick in Phaic Tan the best thing to do is phone home and confirm that you have made a will. For the more optimistic, ask your **hotel concierge** to recommend a doctor. Resist any offers by reception desk staff to deal with the problem themselves as their medical skills are generally **sub-standard** and often attract high charges.

In the event of requiring hospital treatment, there are reasonable facilities in Bumpattabumpah as well as most provincial centres. The best **emergency health care** can usually be found at one of Phaic Tan's military hospitals although to gain admission it may be necessary to inflict a **bullet wound**.

For those who prefer **alternative health care**, the northern city of Nham Pong also boasts a 24-hour witch doctor clinic. Here patients can receive a magical incantation or **protective amulet** at any time of the day.

Note *Many hospitals in Phaic Tan are under-equipped and it is not unusual for patients requiring an X-ray to be sent to the nearest airport where they can pass through a baggage-screening device.*

Tina Writes...
For the Cautious Traveller

Despite claims that the Phaic Tanese are generally open, honest people, I constantly remind myself that there are bad apples in every bunch. It's better to reject any overtures of friendliness than risk having your trip spoilt by dishonest behaviour that you should have seen coming.

Many Phaic Tanese cardiovascular surgeons prefer working in outdoor operating theatres.

Safety

Although Phaic Tan is in no way a dangerous country to visit, there are certain obvious **precautions** you can take to avoid problems. Most hotels have large safes – you might consider sleeping in one. If going out alone after dark, let the concierge know so he can stop you. In the larger cities petty crimes such as pick-pocketing and arson are on the rise but further afield the most you're likely to encounter is the **occasional occasional blow-dart** to the back of the neck.

Should you find yourself the victim of a crime while in Phaic Tan report it to the local police unless it's murder in which case you'll need someone else to do it for you. One word of warning – some **female travellers** seeking police help have described being asked personal and – in some cases – quite improper questions by local law enforcement offices. Be warned – a complete medical examination is not a necessary step when reporting a missing wallet.

Drugs

Despite its past image as something of a pot smoker's paradise, Phaic Tan has got tough on illegal drug taking with **stiff penalties** now in place. Anyone caught with 'unlawful substances' can expect to find themselves spending several years either in **gaol** or teaching English as a second language.

Tina Writes...
For the Cautious Traveller

Nothing attracts unwanted attention more quickly than opening a map on a busy street corner. Before you know it you'll be deluged by locals offering help and, while some of these may be genuine, I take no chances. It's better to spend the day lost and wandering aimlessly for hours than to fall victim to some tout's wily charms.

MARCHING ORDERS
Travel anywhere in Phaic Tan and you're likely to see members of the military wandering about in their distinctive uniforms. Highly professional and with a proud history of battle, Phaic Tanese soldiers have always struggled to maintain a fierce image, a result of them being the only fighting unit in the world to wear sarongs into battle.

Phaic Tan's first east-meets-west lavatory.

Toilets

Toilets, or as they're known in Phaic Tanese, *lo sqot*, can take a bit of getting used to. Set flush to the ground, the left leg is placed on a **raised footpad** while the right leg remains tucked back at a 45 degree angle. And that's just urinating. In rural areas toilets are more basic still, often consisting of just a few **planks** over a hole in the floor. Whilst this arrangement works well enough for the owners, it's not pleasant living in the apartment below.

Smoking

Phaic Tan is generally considered a nicotine addict's paradise, with very few restrictions on where one may light up, although there are moves to phase out smoking in **childcare centres** and intensive care wards. Bowing to World Health Organization pressure, the Government has also declared it illegal for shopkeepers to sell tobacco products to anyone under the age of 16 unless they are able to produce the correct money. Those eating out should be warned: there is no such thing as 'non-smoking' in Phaic Tanese restaurants. Only top-end establishments are likely to have a **smoke-free section** and chances are it'll be one table out back near the gents.

In some parts of the country it is illegal to light up within 1m of another person.

Laundry

Most hotels provide guest laundry services although caution should be exercised as **commercial laundries** in Phaic Tan use a very powerful starch (technically a fabric hardener) that has been known to cause **skin abrasions** and, in one incident, severe lacerations, when a visitor in a newly washed shirt attempted to look over his shoulder.

Customs & Visas

Before arriving in Phaic Tan you will need to apply for a visa. This process can take several weeks and be quite complicated so it is worth getting an agent to handle the paper work.

Warning: there are some **disreputable agents** operating within Phaic Tan and prospective travellers should be suspicious of any requests for a passport photo involving you or your travelling partner in **lingerie**.

Like most countries, Phaic Tan prohibits the importation of certain goods such as drugs, firearms, bathroom air-freshener and motor vehicle mufflers.

X-Rated

Those bringing **pornographic material** into the country should be prepared to declare it and, in some cases, make photocopies for the customs staff. Similarly, X-rated video tapes will be confiscated by officials from the Culture and Information Department and not returned until they have been screened at their New Year's Eve party.

Clothing and toiletries for personal use are allowed in duty free and visitors may arrive with up to 1 litre of alcohol, either in bottles or their bloodstream.

Phaic Tan has strict **quarantine regulations**, so you are not allowed to bring pets unless they are for personal consumption.

Traveller's Tip

It is unwise to jog in Phaic Tanese cities as the local police tend to open fire at anything moving faster than walking pace.

Tina Writes...
For the Cautious Traveller

Money Management is an essential part of crime-proofing yourself. If I've got, say, $200 in cash I leave $190 in my hotel safe, taking with me the key and a photographic record of the contents. The remaining $10 I distribute in various places: $3 in my left shoe, $2.50 in a money belt (a separate empty money belt is then placed over this as a decoy) and the remaining $4.50 worth of coins is sewn into the underwiring of my bra ensuring not only security but a firm figure.

Photography

Photographic equipment and supplies are readily available throughout Phaic Tan. Most of the larger cities have labs that can process, print and lose your film within two hours.

Remember that in certain regularly visited areas **tribespeople** will expect money if you photograph them. In heavily touristed areas they may demand **payment** simply for looking in their direction. If in doubt, remember the universal rule of travel: smile and wave some **US currency**.

Photographer's Tip

As Phaic Tan is a tropical country photographers might find it useful putting some silica gel inside their camera case to prevent the growth of mould. A similar strategy works well in underpants.

Electricity

The electric current in Phaic Tan varies from region to region. In most of the big cities it is 540 volts. Even with an **adaptor** don't be surprised if your electric shaver starts to glow. In outlying areas the supply trickles down to as low as 50 volts.

Criminals in these parts of Phaic Tan sentenced to the electric chair have ended up dying from deep vein thrombosis and in some cases car batteries are used to speed the process up.

Electrical wiring can be somewhat complicated in Phaic Tan as every household appliance runs on a different voltage.

Philippe Writes...

For me, travel is a serious business and you'll never get much out of a trip if you let enjoyment get in the way. Why run round taking endless shots with digital cameras when, for twice the effort, you can carry a complete set of water-colours and bulky sketch-pad?

Disabled Travellers

Phaic Tan has made considerable improvements in this area and disabled visitors will be pleased to now find a **wheelchair ramp** installed at Phlat Chat airport. Make the most of this facility though – it's the only one in the country.

Travelling with Children

You should have no concerns about taking young children to Phaic Tan as the locals love kids and will often stop to pat or poke them. Children can also come in handy; if, for example, you plan on hiring a motorbike one can be left as a **deposit**.

WARNING _Some hotels and resorts claim to offer 'Kids' Clubs'. In many cases this phrase can be misleading and parents should be especially wary if asked whether their children are members of the Textile Workers' Union._

Money

The basic unit of currency in Phaic Tan is the **P'ting**, a name believed to derive from the sound this coin makes when hitting a cash register tray. There are 100 P'tings to the P'tong. At the airport in Bumpattabumpah or in most hotels and banks you'll be able to change foreign currency for P'ting or glass beads, depending on **exchange rates**.

Banks

Banks are generally open Monday through Friday except for days when their **safety deposit boxes** have been cleaned out by armed bandits (often a Thursday). There are very few ATMs in the country and visitors are advised against asking for the nearest 'hole in the wall' unless you are looking for a **public toilet**.

The rare 'double chin' version of the Phaic Tanese gold coin is extremely valuable. On the King's insistence, a more 'faithful' representation of the Queen's profile appeared on later coins.

Apart from the official **Government bank** (the Federal Bank of Phaic Tan) a few smaller financial institutions have recently sprung up including the Phaic Tanese Para-military Building Society (PTPBS), the only bank in the world where tellers have been known to hold up their customers. Several **private operators** have also set up shop in the country, most run by ex-Hong Kong financiers. The largest of these is the RRTB (Royal Rogue Traders' Bank).

Phaic Tan's national bank – voted 'Most Robbed Financial Institution' in the world.

Communications

Phaic Tan has a modern, well-maintained **telephone system** linking most parts of the country. Note that within the next year all seven-digit telephone numbers will be replaced by eight-digit ones. The change has been called for by **Royal Numerologists**.

Internet communication has been slow coming to Phaic Tan, not helped by the Information Ministry's attempts to monitor and restrict access to 'inappropriate' web sites via a filter that automatically removes any references to sex, drugs, terrorism or the Queen's weight. E-mail is notoriously slow and most people within Phaic Tan prefer receiving messages via **carrier pigeon** as the birds are not only more reliable, they're edible.

Standard internet pointer

Phaic Tanese internet pointer

Philippe Writes... Don't start me on internet cafes!

Postal services are quite good although be warned that parcels, particularly large ones, will routinely be opened and the contents checked by **customs officials**. This precaution follows a wave of attempts during the 1990s by locals to avoid expensive airline tickets by mailing their relatives overseas.

Note *When sending a package out of Phaic Tan post office fees are not calculated according to weight, rather how much string you have used.*

EMERGENCY NUMBERS	
In an emergency, you can call:	
FIRE	590
POLICE	591
AMBULANCE	595
MASSAGE	777

Philippe Writes... Alright then. I cannot stand them. When I first started travelling it was a simple fact that you would be out of contact with home for possibly months on end. Maybe the odd postcard would be sent but beyond that there was no communication. And that's the way we liked it. I was away for much of the 70s and during that time my parents weren't even sure if I was alive. What's more, they didn't seem to care. Nowadays you see these would-be backpackers lined up in the nearest internet café sending home hourly accounts of their tedious trip. In my opinion, if you make contact with family or friends more than once every six weeks then you're not travelling.

Adoption

Visitors interested in adopting a Phaic Tanese child should be warned that the process is **extremely rigorous** and virtually impossible to negotiate unless you are acting for an established international aid agency, a UN humanitarian relief program or a Hollywood star. Remember, too, that the Phaic Tanese definition of 'child' does not always match our own and couples yearning for a baby may well find themselves accepting delivery of a 46-year-old rice farmer (right).

A Phaic Tanese children's home, circa 1963. Fortunately times have moved on from when infants could be forcibly removed from their parents for failing to have properly bleached clothes.

OVERSEAS AID ORGANIZATIONS

The following is a list of government and non-government organizations you might come across during your stay in Phaic Tan.

Field Safe – a UK-based NGO committed to de-mining the country.

BVRP – a Vietnamese-funded organization intent on re-mining de-mined areas.

Medecins Sans Frontieres – a committed group of international medical practitioners providing aid and assistance.

Medecins Sans Penicillin – a team of heavily under-funded doctors.

Medecins Sans Pantalons – a little known group of Belgian beer enthusiasts. Just avoid.

(Left) Many Phaic Tanese street vendors wear masks to protect themselves from traffic fumes as well as the smell rising up from their own produce.

Where to Stay

The range and quality of accommodation in Phaic Tan has improved enormously over recent years but many establishments still struggle to meet western standards. At the top end, you can expect all the luxuries of home but towards the budget end things may get a little primitive. As a general rule, the grander a hotel's title, the more wary you should be. Examples include The Royal Opulence (a youth hostel in Kaipoc), The Grand Imperial (bungalow-style accommodation used by itinerant labourers on the west coast) and Bumpattabumpah's Royal Majestic Country Club Resort (an outer city leper colony).

All hotels in Phaic Tan are either privately owned or state-run. The latter tend to be cold and unfriendly with many of the staff actually medium-security prisoners serving out the remainder of their sentences in the hospitality industry.

Note Many top hotels in Phaic Tan boast satellite TV such as BBC, CNN and ESPN but beware, this often means that the channels have been taped illegally somewhere else and played a few days later on the in-house video system.

Sven Writes...
For the Budget Traveller

Never, and I mean never, accept the published room rate. Demand to see the duty manager and ask about stand-by specials, or seasonal discounts. If none are offered then discuss the possibility of an extra-early check-out time – often worth a 20% rate cut. Tell the manager you're willing to take a room without windows or share a suite with a family who have a bed to spare. Even if none of these options work out, by this time it will be morning and you'll no longer require a room.

Top Tip #1

As a rule, be wary of any hotel boasting 'local charm'. This is generally accepted as a euphemism for 'concrete latrine'.

In this Jetlag guide we use the following hotel ratings.

Luxury: hot and cold filtered water, a/c, private bathrooms, obsequious staff.

Mid Range: very basic, outdoor toilets, no a/c

Budget: should only be considered if seeking shelter from a typhoon

Credit Card Abbreviations

AE	American Express
DC	Diners Club
MC	Master Card
V	Visa
CO	Cash Only
OD	Or Drugs

Accommodation standards vary widely throughout Phaic Tan, from basic backpacker-style cabins (top) through to luxurious beachfront bures (above) where, if the end of your toilet paper isn't folded into a perfect triangle within five minutes of use, the entire house-keeping staff will be sacked on the spot.

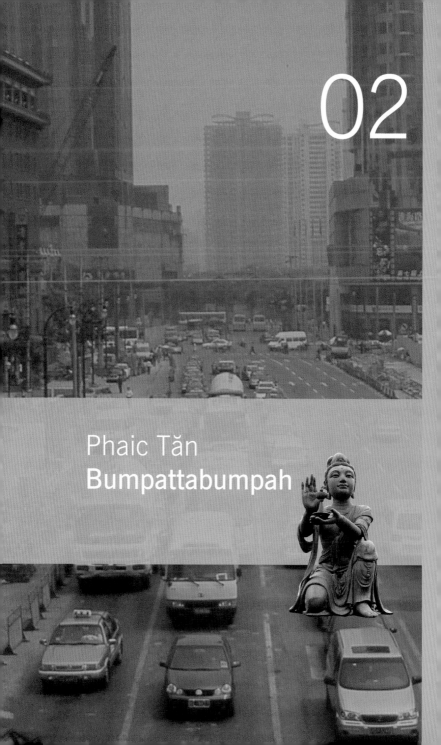

02

Phaic Tăn
Bumpattabumpah

Introduction

From the moment you arrive in Phaic Tan's capital Bumpattabumpah, the place will grip your senses. Streets throb with **traffic**, most of it ambulances en route to the latest **multi-car collision**. The French style ornate buildings, many headquarters for local aid agencies, sit alongside traditional **bamboo bungalows** set on traditional stilts made of PVC piping. On each corner, street vendors fill the air with **savoury smells**, as does their food. And everywhere there are people bustling about – businessmen with cell phones pressed to their ear, schoolgirls in starched white uniforms and serene, **saffron-robed monks** fighting over whose windscreen they should be cleaning.

The capital of Phaic Tan is a bustling, sprawling city in the south east of the country. Its name actually means 'water convergence' and refers to the fact that the city is situated where the country's main river, the mighty Pong meets untreated effluent from a **sewage treatment plant** upstream. From here it flows into the Kut River which then branches off into the lower Kut and the upper Kut. Bumpattabumpah was originally known as Phxux Xauan, its name only changed in 1933 when a survey revealed that less than 12% of the population were capable of pronouncing it.

City of Contrasts

A city of contrasts, Bumpattabumpah boasts some of the wealthiest and poorest people in Phaic Tan. Downtown you'll find **luxury apartments** and semi authentic designer shops such as Luigi Vuitton. It was here as recently as 1997 that developers announced plans to build the tallest office block in the world. Construction actually started but shortly after the foundations were dug the **Asian economic crisis** hit, meaning the project was shelved. Bumpattabumpah now boasts the largest unfenced hole in the ground.

Quality of Life

Of course, head out from the city centre and you'll soon come to the slums and **shanty towns** of Bumpattabumpah. The quality of life for people here is poor with basic services such as water, sewerage and electricity lacking. Garbage collection, where it exists, involves bins being picked up in one street and then dumped in the next, more a **re-location service** than refuse disposal.

High smog levels in Bumpattabumpah mean that office tower blocks require no window tinting.

Little goes to waste in Phaic Tan. Following the launch failure of their Asia-PT1 satellite, innovative technicians converted it into a functional street-sweeper.

(Left) A boat load of tourists make their way up the mighty Pong under the skillful control of a colourfully dressed Ihosmay ('escaped convict').

Orientation

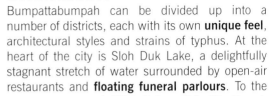

Bumpattabumpah can be divided up into a number of districts, each with its own **unique feel**, architectural styles and strains of typhus. At the heart of the city is Sloh Duk Lake, a delightfully stagnant stretch of water surrounded by open-air restaurants and **floating funeral parlours**. To the

east of Sloh Duk you'll find the French Quarter (or *Quartier Française*) with its colonial architecture (*architecture colonialle*), stately, tree-lined boulevards (*boulevards aux arbres*) and tendency to use reverse adjectives (*adjectifs reversés*). The south of the city is the industrial sector with smoke belching factories, hazardous waste dumps and **cargo depots** packed side by side. This is also its residential district.

Getting an Overview

A good way of getting your bearings is to take a bus ride to the top of **Mount Phahoc** although the road is so windy that many people lose their bearings, along with their lunch. But once recovered you can enjoy a magnificent view out across the city from the observation tower. Admission is 500p and while some visitors have complained that the panoramic vista is frequently obscured by **heavy smog**, its worth remembering that poor visibility will mean you'll be protected from snipers and at the same time getting a clear view of what happens when the **Kyoto Protocol** is not adhered to.

HEALTH ALERT!

Pollution levels in Bumpa-ttabumpah have soared as a result of the construction boom: dust from demolition, piling, bricks and tiles along with sand blown from the backs of trucks add an estimaed 200cu of pollutants to the urban atmosphere every day. For this reason, anyone suffering from asthma or related lung conditions should refrain from breathing in between the hours of 8.00am and 6.00pm weekdays.

DID YOU KNOW?

In Bumpattabumpah's Old City many of the original houses were built of bricks 'cemented' together with sugar-cane juice, a construction practice that served residents well until the **Great Famine of 1763** when hordes of hungry peasants desperate for food ate a large section of the neighbourhood.

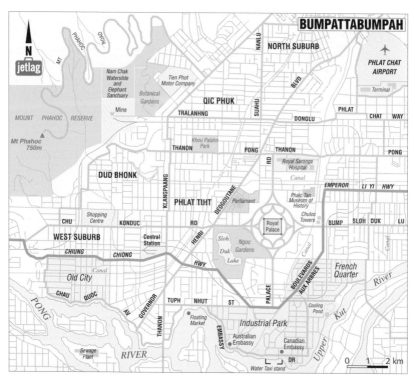

Homeless people living along the canals of Bumpattabumpah benefit from food distribution programs such as this one, Meals on Keels.

History

Somewhere between 350,000 and 800,000 years ago a distant ancestor of modern man, homo flacidus settled in the southern valleys of Phaic Tan. Fossilized bones of these **ancient tree dwellers** have turned up in various archaeological digs as well as an inner-city restaurant that has subsequently been closed down. How the precise location of Bumpattabumpah was chosen remains lost in history but legend has it that sometime during the 3rd century **Emperor Li Yi** was looking for a place to build his new palace and so he placed a relic on a sacred **white elephant** who was then allowed to wander freely through the hills. The elephant climbed to the top of Mt Phahoc and down the other side towards the River Pong where he was speared by a poacher. The palace was built on this spot. Shortly after this Emperor Yi married a local princess Phuydana, creating a powerful dynasty that united the region. Their marriage portrait is believed to be depicted in a **stone carving** just north of the city and nearby, archaeologists recently uncovered one of the original wedding gifts, a bronze toaster. With the end of the Yi dynasty Bumpattabumpah fell into a period of **lawlessness** as rival tribes fought for control of the region. Armed bandits such as the infamous Ngam Chua also roamed freely, terrorising the population.

HEIRLESS

Despite being married to Emperor Yi for many years, Phuydana failed to produce an heir to the throne and the Emperor was forced to take other wives, 104 in all, but none fell pregnant, a situation later blamed on overly tight royal undergarments.

A Spanish account of Bumpattabumpah (circa 1605)

This account of Bumpattabumpah is taken from an anonymous manuscript compiled by a Spanish missionary who visited the city during the 17th century.

'The region is thickly populated with lithe, smiling folk who appear to be in a constant state of civil unrest. Violent outbursts are common even amongst members of the one family. The people do not eat anything properly cooked, but only in raw or putrid condition; and in order to digest these foods they are great drinkers of very strong spirits. They divide their year into six festivals, during the first of which the vast majority pay tribute to the king. During the second festival the king is assassinated amidst great rejoicing and drink. Drinking remains the dominate theme of the next three festivals. The year ends with a massive tiger hunt in which young men from surrounding villages prove their bravery by each clubbing to death a litter of cubs. Then they go drinking.'

Known as the 'Robin Hood of Bumpattabumpah' this audacious criminal stole from both the rich and the poor, in the belief that he didn't want to be seen showing favouritism. A series of **famines** afflicted the area during the 18th century and thousands of people starved to death. Others just managed to survive on a meagre diet of rice and **Jesuit missionaries**.

When the French invaded Phaic Tan in 1690 Bumpattabumpah soon found itself surrounded by heavily armed troops. The city's then Emperor Chiung Chiong urged his subjects to take up arms and fight to the death but his subjects weren't so keen on the idea, agreeing instead that they would fight to 5:30pm and then re-assess the situation. Within hours a white flag was raised and the French stormed in. During the ensuing period of **colonial rule** Bumpattabumpah was greatly expanded and numerous buildings constructed including the magnificent Opera House (the *Sung Phlat*), one of the finest public structures in Bumpattabumpah. Building began in 1702 when workers drove some 40,000 bamboo piles into the mud of the River Pong to provide foundations. The poles sank without trace and it was decided instead to drive the workers into the mud. The resulting structure, home to Phaic Tan's **National Opera Company** has stood proudly ever since, untroubled by fire, flood, monsoon storms, civil war or, for most of the time, audiences.

HONOURABLE HENRI...

Wander the streets of Bumpattabumpah and you will very quickly come across references to former French Governor Henri Deogoutane. There are statues, streets, parks, public urinals, desserts, insects and even a massage parlour named in memory of this colonial overlord. Born in Marseilles in 1863 to an aristocratic family, Deogoutane was destined for a distinguished  military career until illness struck. Doctors diagnosed gout and told him to cut down on drinking, news that hit the 12-year-old pretty hard. But Deogoutane conquered this affliction and went on to study philosophy and torture in Paris. When war came, like so many other young men, he lied about his age, claiming to be 16. But the truth was soon exposed and the dashing 27-year-old cavalry officer found himself posted to Phaic Tan as provincial governor. He went on to rule the city with a firm yet psychopathic hand for almost two decades during which time he survived over 40 assassination attempts, including several from his own parish priest. In 1910 Henri Deogoutane died peacefully in his sleep surrounded by his family – they smothered him with a pillow.

The Great Resistance

By the early stages of the 20th century resistance to French rule was beginning to grow. Translations of works by Engels and social Darwinists found their way into the hands of the Phaic Tanese intelligentsia, both of whom read them with interest. Early protests against French rule initially took the form of low-key **civil disobedience**; in 1908 a large number of local civil servants and government employees instigated a city-wide strike, designed to throw the regime into chaos. The strike was only abandoned after six months when it became obvious that no one had noticed it was taking place.

But in 1912 a young Bumpattabumpahn visionary emerged to galvanize the resistance movement. Chau Quoc (1882–1947) wrote numerous tracts calling for the French to be expelled and urging his fellow countrymen to rise up in armed revolt. 'Fear not the danger,' Quoc wrote in one of his more **fiery treatises**, 'for no sacrifice is too great to see our beloved land free from the colonial aggressor'. Brave words indeed, no less potent for the fact that Chau Quoc was at this point hiding with relatives in Bali.

With opposition to French rule growing, Quoc was eventually persuaded to return home and help co-ordinate a **guerilla campaign**. He formed the TKR (People's Military Force) and set about harassing colonial authorities. Things reached a head in 1914 when a provincial tax official was beaten to death with a baguette and the TKR were forced to flee the city.

From their base in the nearby Nha Bhin Mountains Quoc and his band of insurgents would regularly ambush French troops with mixed results as their **brightly coloured sarongs** often gave their position away. This, coupled with the TKR boasting some of the most short-sighted snipers in military history, limited the effectiveness of their campaign. But Quoc refused to be deterred and in 1916 he led his troops back into the city on what became known as the 'Long March'. The actual distance was less than 6km but, ever the brilliant strategist, Quoc surprised everyone by taking the **scenic route**, a tactic that paid off when the TKR stormed the city unopposed and routed the French. Several weeks later Chau Quoc proclaimed the creation of the **Democratic People's Republic of Phaic Tan** with himself as supreme, eternal dictator for life.

THE PEOPLE'S HERO

Surprisingly little is known about the life of Chau Quoc, the man generally regarded as the father of Phaic Tanese independence. Born in 1882, the son of Bumpattabumpah merchants, he traveled overseas to Europe at the age of 16 where he first came across communist ideology. After reading the works of Marx, Lenin and Trotsky he was filled with a vision – to one day grow a beard – and returned home full of revolutionary fervour. A reputedly handsome man, Quoc received numerous offers of marriage but refused all, saying he was too committed to the revolution to take a wife of his own. This didn't stop him taking other men's wives and estimates suggest that almost 30% of TKR party members were personally fathered by Quoc. A philosopher, revolutionary, communist and humanitarian, Quoc was also a staunch proponent of feminism, believing fervently that women should be allowed to join the workforce. Fittingly, he died in a Bumpattabumpah brothel.

After Quoc's death Bumpattabumpah became the centre of numerous battles between communist and pro-democracy forces with neither side ever quite able to gain the ascendancy. The city again hit international headlines during the 1950s when several Buddhist monks set themselves on fire as a protest against government corruption and human rights abuses. The first holy man to self-immolate was Kem Duc Ke, although opinion remains divided as to whether he was protesting or simply the victim of a faulty gas barbecue fitting.

There is no doubt that years of battles and civil unrest have left their mark on Bumpattabumpah, from its artillery-damaged buildings to its **heavily armed population**. Even the city's pedestrian lights reflect past conflicts, with a stationary red man indicating 'do not cross' and a crouching green figure denoting 'make a dash for cover'. But for all its bloody past, Bumpattabumpah today is a modern, bustling metropolis on the go. Despite **infrastructure problems** commerce is booming; Bumpattabumpah currently ranks as the world's number one producer of **car fragrances** and that green plastic grass served with sushi. Its public hospital continues to pioneer **ground-breaking advances** in medical research; doctors at Royal Bumpattabumpah recently managed to join two non-Siamese twins at the head.

In 1993 Bumpattabumpah entered into a sister city relationship with Danang in Vietnam, a relationship that lasted until 1998 when the two towns declared war on each other.

Crime

Sadly, Bumpattabumpah has developed something of a reputation for **petty crime** and theft. The most common form involves young men on fast motorcycles who cruise the streets waiting for unwary victims. These thieves commonly snatch bags (*right*), necklaces, watches, hair-pieces, expensive underwear and – in one recently reported incident – a **fully functional pace-maker**. There has also been a spate of armed robberies throughout the city in which criminals have held up banks armed with a syringe full of local water.

Tina Writes...
For the Cautious Traveller
The key is to not look too wealthy. I see so many tourists wandering about, flashing video cameras and jewellery. In contrast, I dress as a destitute or cripple with a hacking cough and unwashed hair. In particularly dangerous places I may even visibly wet my pants. Sightseeing might take a little longer on crutches but you won't become an easy target.

Getting There

Most visitors to Bumpattabumpah will fly in on board a Royal Fok Tok passenger service and land at Phlat Chat Airport or, if winds are strong, within several kilometres of it. Shortly after take-off passengers will be sprayed with an **aerosol insecticide** designed to reduce the risk of introducing pests into the country. It also helps mask any smell from the **on-board toilets**.

Phlat Chat Airport lacks an air bridge and passengers will be driven from their aircraft to the terminal by bus. Expect the journey to take upwards of two hours as the driver will generally insist on stopping en route at a variety of shops owned by 'relatives' and only when sufficient **souvenirs** have been purchased will you be permitted to reach the arrivals lounge.

The airport itself is situated some 19km from the city centre. A taxi ride from the airport into town should cost around 3000p, more if you expect to ride inside the vehicle.

Ballroom dancing classes are popular in Bumpattabumpah. Students without a partner may practise with a bike.

Bumpattabumpah boasts some of the shortest firemen in Southeast Asia.

Sven Writes...
For the Budget Traveller

Taxis and tuk-tuks from Bumpattabumpah airport into town can be a little pricey so your best bet is to go by bus. There's no direct service, but if you're prepared to change lines several times and complete the final 3km on foot it's possible to do the trip for under 200p (about US 7 cents).

Getting Round

First time visitors to Bumpattabumpah are invariably struck by the sheer volume of traffic moving along its streets. Overcrowded roads, combined with the widespread belief that it is unlucky to turn left, lead to general **chaos** and everywhere you look there are near misses and blatant examples of **reckless driving**. The fact that Phaic Tanese citizens may legally drive at 12 only adds to the general chaos.

Taxis

Taxis are probably your best option for getting round Bumpattabumpah and drivers are easily identified by their **colourful vests** and extensive skin abrasions.

Fares vary widely and it's worth agreeing on a price before your journey starts as Bumpattabumpahn taxi drivers will often not turn the meter on. Unfortunately, the same reluctance does not extend to their radios, and the ear-splitting sound of Rice FM will often be a feature of your trip.

Remember that most taxis leave for their destination when the vehicle is full. It's not uncommon for there to be up to seven passengers squeezed inside, including an extra person between the driver and the door, someone curled up where the **spare wheel** should be and a small child wedged behind the radiator. The glove compartment may also contain livestock.

Due to the high incidence of breakdowns, Bumpattabumpahn taxi drivers generally prefer to travel in convoy.

Trishaws

For those on a tight budget, consider taking a trishaw (a taxi missing one wheel) which will often be a **cheaper**, if somewhat more wobbly, option.

Cyclos

An even less expensive and, some would say, more authentic means of getting around the city is in a cyclo. Something like a **reverse rickshaw**, the customer sits in the front and the driver pedals from behind. The only downside is that in the event of a head-on collision you cease being a passenger and officially become an **air-bag**. Within the city cyclos will take you door to door for just 4000p. Expect to pay extra if you want that door to be your own.

Dokars

The most traditional form of transport in Bumpattabumpah, dokars are **ox-driven carts** that can often be seeing plying shorter routes within the inner city. Dokars are a surprisingly convenient form of transportation and generally cheap. Fares are negotiated directly with the ox.

Hire Cars

Driving yourself is not advisable in Bumpattabumpah due to the sheer volume of traffic and complexity of **local road rules**. Some streets are designated two-way at certain times of the day but then change to one-way without any obvious sign except for the over-laden lorry heading straight for you. Parking can also be a **nightmare** and around certain city areas such as railway stations strict no-standing laws apply. Drivers in breach can expect to find a homeless person clamped to their wheel.

In recent years there have also been regular reports of police stopping tourists for supposed driving infringements and 'fining' them in what is essentially an **extortion racket**. The usual giveaway is that the officers involved will demand the fine be only paid with foreign currency or cigarettes.

Philippe Writes...
I scoff at mindless tourists taking expensive taxis with their air-conditioned comfort and tinted window view of the world. For me, the more traditional and grass roots the transportation the better. I once paid a one-lunged peasant 500p to peddle me up Mount Phahoc on the back of his cyclo. Yes, the 5km trip took longer than it might have in a cab but over the course of our three-day ascent I experienced the real Phaic Tan. Priceless.

Tina Writes...
For the Cautious Traveller

I've heard so many stories of gullible tourists done over by disreputable motorbike dealers. The scam works like this. You are forced to leave your passport as security when hiring a motorbike. An hour or two later your hired bike is then conveniently 'stolen' and the owner – surprise surprise – demands big money or else no passport. Now before I hire, I accuse every bike store owner of being a cheat and threaten to call the police. Genuine traders will become very distressed and even teary, pleading their innocence. You can then hire the bike in safety knowing that a veiled threat still hangs in the air.

Motorcycles

If you insist on driving yourself then hiring a motorcycle might be the best option for getting round the city. You'll need to produce an international drivers' licence although many motorcycle hire agencies will also accept a **clearly visible tattoo**.

By law rental agencies are obliged to supply a helmet but this will often be a home-made version, constructed out of spray-painted egg cartons. There have been numerous reports of **unsafe motorbikes** offered for hire in Bumpattabumpah. Before riding check carefully the state of the bike – anything with less than two wheels should be treated with caution.

Remember that Phaic Tanese drive on the left-hand side of the road except for the period leading up to a **full moon** at which time the right lane is considered more auspicious. The middle is always a safe bet.

Bikes

Whilst cheap, bicycles are not recommended within the city as cyclists have least priority on the road, and must give way to everything including pedestrians, food carts, stray dogs and chickens. You may, however, legally pull out in front of leg-less beggars on skateboards.

Rail

In 1996, Bumpattabumpah proudly unveiled its new 'Sky Rail' service – a 15km overhead loop around the city. Sadly, many of the supporting columns holding up the track collapsed during monsoon rains and sections of the Sky Rail are now technically an **underground railway**. More reliable is Bumpattabumpah's standard railway system that links pretty much all parts of the city. Using the service is quite easy. A rail pass may be obtained at any station from an automatic ticketing machine. When purchasing tickets make sure you have the right change and remember it is considered polite to tip the machine. Access to the platform is gained via automated turnstiles. Insert your ticket and the turnstile barriers will open. Do not hesitate passing through as several **slow commuters** have suffered a badly crushed pelvis. Platforms are clearly marked and trains leave for most destinations every 10 minutes. Shortly before leaving the station you will hear a short, high-pitched noise indicating either that the train is about to start moving or that the conductor has got his foot caught in the door.

TICKET TO RIDE
Many automated ticket machines in Phaic Tan require you to haggle. Here is how it works. The machine will demand 100p. Press the button marked 20p. The machine will counter offer, somewhere between 60–80p. Lift your offer to 40p. If it sticks to 70p or above, pretend to walk away or try your luck with another machine.

Buses

There are two types of bus in Bumpattabumpah, private and government owned. **Government buses** are generally cheaper as they don't have air-conditioning or, in many cases, an adult driver. To catch a government bus simply stand by the road and wait for one to break down. **Private buses** are a better option for longer cross-town trips and tickets may be purchased on board. There are **three classes** of travel but third class is technically reserved for students or passengers bringing deceased loved-ones home for burial.

Traveller's Tip

Fares on Bumpatta-bumpahn buses and trains are often calculated, not on distance, but on how much of a seat you are taking up. Inspectors armed with calipers and tape measures regularly patrol. Remember also, when riding any form of public transport in Bumpattabumpah, to give up your seat to the elderly, infirm or anyone carrying a gun.

Shopping

While Bumpattabumpah may not be the shopping capital of Southeast Asia there are plenty of opportunities for the determined bargain hunter, especially if you're in the market for **commemorative spoons**, radio-controlled toys or brightly coloured plastic buckets.

Perhaps the greatest attraction is the many **excellent tailors** located within the city, all of whom are capable of producing skirts, shirts and jackets within a very short period of time. Obviously, with such strict time restraints the quality can vary and in many cases hems may be **glued** rather than stitched, but the workmanship is surprisingly good.

If for any reason you can't get out and about, it's still possible to enjoy a bit of 'retail therapy' courtesy of Bumpattabumpah's cable TV Shopping Network. Similar to the US version this is the only TV shopping network in which potential buyers can phone in and haggle.

Philippe Writes...

I have to laugh at tourists heading off like cattle on packaged tours to big shopping malls. The last time I was in Bumpattabumpah I got chatting to a cab driver whose brother just happened to own a jewellery shop. It's normally closed to foreigners but he agreed to open it for me and when we got there we discovered they just happened to be in the middle of a major stocktaking sale. While those gullible fools were off wasting money in some faceless shopping centre I was picking up genuine quartz for just US$55 a kilo. Ha!

A customer at a downtown tailor's shop is measured for a new suit, blissfully unaware that his trousers have just been stolen.

Lacquerware

Lacquerware is also plentiful and cheap although Bumpattabumpah craftsmen use a particularly dense – and therefore heavy – varnish which may lead to **excess baggage penalties** when you fly out. On the plus side, if you're going diving off the east coast even the smallest trinket makes an excellent **weight belt**.

Weekend Market

A great place to pick up a bargain is at Bumpattabumpah's famous weekend market (closed Saturday afternoon and Sunday). Thousands of stall holders offer everything from **traditional handicrafts** to cut price ammonium nitrate (used as a breath freshener). There's an entire pavilion devoted to **antiques**, many of which are manufactured on site, and even if you don't intend to buy anything the markets are a great place to wander around and have your **wallet** stolen.

The popular endangered species section of Bumpattabumpah's weekend market.

Tina Writes...
For the Cautious Traveller

When shopping, never let your credit card out of your sight. A common scam goes like this. The shopkeeper takes your card and pretends to 'swipe' it under the counter where accomplice number one lies on a specially designed shelf ready to write down the number and pass it on to accomplice number three (accomplice number two is often just a decoy) who heads next door and buys up half a ton of chemical fertilizer in your name. I've seen it happen before and for this reason I always insist on swiping my own card and then immediately swallowing the paper imprint.

Where to Stay

There has been an enormous number of hotels built and renovated within Bumpattabumpah over the past decade and as a result you will have little trouble finding both accommodation and construction sites. Because of the over supply many establishments now offer incentives, including free breakfast and topless check-in, and it's worth asking about discount offers. The most exclusive (and therefore most expensive) hotels tend to be along the riverfront and upwind of the rice wine distillery. Remember – all hotels in Bumpattabumpah are obliged to charge a 7% service levy, 10% value-added tax (VAT) and a 12% protection fee to avoid becoming the target of an arson attack.

$$$$ Criminally Expensive

✉ *313 Thanon Pong*
☎ *33 932 834*
@ *orient@phoni.com.pt*
▤ *MC V*
  topless check-in

The Orient Star Considered by many to be one of the finest hotels in Southeast Asia, the Orient overlooks the mighty Pong and from its spacious balconies guests can watch overloaded passanger ferries capsize while sipping a complimentary cocktail. Guests traditionally arrive in stretch limos or on board the Orient's custom-made wooden barges to be greeted by silk clad staff showering the lobby with orchid petals. A full massage service is provided while you check in and a string quartet plays live inside each of the elevators. There are wide screen televisions in every room and the mini bar comes with its own live-in cocktail waiter.

✉ *78 Tralanhng Donglu*
☎ *33 583 089*
@ *royal@phalti.com.pt*
▤ *DC MC V*

The Royal Krahvat is another of Bumpattabumpah's grander hotels, offering the ultimate in extravagance and luxury. The hotel boasts more than 700 Viennese chandeliers, lush Tai Ping carpets, artistic flower arrangements and numerous priceless artworks. Unfortunately, due to security concerns, these are all locked inside the manager's office but the lobby is adorned with a magnificent marble fountain that sprays French champagne metres into the air. Guests are greeted by a waiting fruit basket and box of chocolates bearing a card 'Complimentary'. Be warned – this card is the only thing that is complimentary – eating any of the fruit or chocolates will result in a hefty charge being added to your bill.

Note *Cocktails served at the Royal Krahvat's lounge bar are so large they come with real umbrellas.*

Jonathan Writes... *For the Luxury Traveller*
I've always enjoyed staying at the Orient Star. The suite sizes are generous, the staff suitably obsequious and little touches like shampooing your luggage before delivering it to the room put this establishment in a class of its own. If I had to make one criticism, it's that I couldn't find anything to criticize. *Quel dommage!*

$$$ Expensive

Chu Yu is one of Bumpattabumpah's newer hotels, situated just a short walk from the city centre. The lay-out involves an interesting mix of interlacing levels, more the result of foundations subsiding than any deliberate architectural plan, and the rooms all have river views, or at least odours. A plaque in the lobby boasts that Chu Yu has played host to a string of dignitaries including Joseph Conrad and Somerset Maugham although, given that the place was only built in 2001, this claim may not bear close scrutiny.

✉ *974 Tralanhng Donglu*
☎ *33 372 089*
@ *chuyu@phalti.com.pt*
▤ *DC V*

The Dophuong International was originally a 12-storey hotel until the illegal addition of a roof-top pool in 1998 proved the old adage that water finds its own level – in this case, the third floor. The lobby is bright and cheerful with a large glass-enclosed atrium that overlooks a garden terrace featuring what appears to be a water cascade but is in fact a burst pipe. A unique feature of the Dophuong is its resident psychic; open daily from 10.30am to 7pm, she will use a number of international techniques to predict how much you are likely to be over-charged.

✉ *657 Thanon Klangpaang*
☎ *33 121 040*
@ *dop@phalti.com.pt*
▤ *DC MC V*
    resident psychic

@ One of the most hip hotels to open in Bumpattabumpah does not actually have a name, but is represented by the symbol '@'. Designed by a New York architect who also doesn't have a name, @ is famous for not having doors, a feature that was felt might interrupt its sleek lines. As a result, guests must enter through a discretely placed skylight.

✉ *33 Thanon Klangpaang*
☎ *33 121 424*
@ *hotel@@phalti.com.pt*
▤ *DC MC V*

$$ Mid-Range

✉ *23 Suahu Nanlu*
☎ *33 565 000*
@ *pruhok@phalti.com.pt*
▤ *DC V*
  pool
  gym

The Hotel Pruhok describes itself as 'centrally located' which it is if you're looking for a base from which to explore the city's industrial estate. Once considered one of Bumpattabumpah's premier hotels, the Pruhok lost a lot of its charm when a freeway overpass was constructed directly outside its front door. But it's still good value and centrally located with a gym, conference room and a pool that is generally empty of guests, and all too often, water. The impeccable service begins at the front desk, however, it pretty much ends there too.

✉ *65 Suahu Nanlu*
☎ *33 023 575*
▤ *DC MC V*

The Pakphar Grand has long been a favourite of Bumpattabumpah's expatriate community, many of whom are drawn to its reinforced underground car-park during military coups. It's also popular with families who come for a night and end up staying a week, due to the tendency for its doors to jam shut. Bathrooms are a little small in the lower-end rooms but perfectly functional if you don't mind showering in a foetal position.

Sven Writes...
For the Budget Traveller

The lobbies of up-market hotels are often large and quite luxurious. Provided you're discrete and change your hairstyle daily it's possible to spend several nights there before staff notice and have you removed. If possible, sleep in an upright seated position and avoid hanging wet clothes out to dry unless absolutely necessary.

CORRECTION *In our last edition we referred to the Bumpattabumpah Leisure Club as a 'resort'. This was a typographical error. Visitors seeking accommodation in Bumpattabumpah should note that the Leisure Club is better described as a 'last resort'.*

$ Budget

Phut Ngoc Hotel This attractive little gem is one of Bumpattabumpah's best budget choices and is located near the Old Quarter. It's family run (so often closed for funerals) and room prices are based on size and the degree of smoke damage.

✉ *562 Thanon Klangpaan*
☎ *33 868 576*
   carrier pigeon

Another low-cost option close to the city centre is the **Emperor Inn**. Full of rustic charm, from the dirt floors of its lobby right down to the kerosene powered elevator, you're guaranteed a good night's sleep, thanks to the soft beds, wind chimes and carbon monoxide fumes wafting up from the bus depot below.

✉ *54 Tralanhng Donglu*
☎ *33 841 047*
@ *emperor@phoni.com.pt*
▭ *MC*

The Imperial Wok is an affordable, basic hotel just a little further out of town. The rooms all appear impeccably clean thanks, in part, to the dim lighting and the staff couldn't be more friendly if they tried – which they don't. There are no showers but, as most of the over-head plumbing leaks, you'll have little trouble getting wet.

✉ *6685 Suahu Nanlu*

Tran D'Oc has long been popular with backpackers looking for low-cost lodging in downtown Bumpatta-bumpah. The staff are friendly and can help with just about any request, provided it doesn't involve clean sheets or a non-smoking room. There are private suites as well as dormitories, all in reasonable condition. The flowers and furniture are plastic although the cockroaches are decidedly real.

✉ *96 Thanon Klangpaan*
▭ *MC V*

Tina Writes...
For the Cautious Traveller

Hotel security is a big concern and even in expensive rooms locks on the doors can be flimsy or even non-existent. For this reason I never travel overseas without a pair of steel mesh security grilles and padlock.

Where to Eat

Bumpattabumpah offers just about everything for the visiting food lover in search of a fine dining experience. Dozens of up-market restaurants, many featuring **internationally renowned chefs** working there as guests or detainees, produce sumptuous meals nightly. Of course, for many people the easiest option is to dine at your hotel. This combines the convenience of not having to travel far along with the reassuring thought that most hotels have a **resident doctor** on call. To many, the ultimate dining experience in Bumpattabumpah can be found a-top its famous Revolving Restaurant. Featuring undoubtedly the best views in the city, this restaurant is always popular although, following a recent mechanical overhaul, several visitors have reported that the ride can get a little bumpy. As a precaution diners are requested to remain seated during the meal with their seatbelts fastened.

$$$ Very Expensive

✉ *32 Thanon Pong*
☎ *33 927 353*
▤ *MC V*

One of Bumpattabumpah's finest river-front eateries, the ultra elegant **Hharmonie** specializes in fresh seafood. Whole fish and crustaceans can be chosen from the tank simply by pointing, at which point a junior kitchen hand armed with a face mask and pair of barbecue tongs will be bodily flung in. The place is generally crowded but you will almost certainly be able to find a table in the non-smoking section.

✉ *275 Thanon Klangpaan*
☎ *33 756 901*
▤ *DC MC V*

Ho Binh Walking up the wide, wooden staircase framed by thick, velvet curtains and ornate light fittings you could be forgiven for thinking you were entering an expensive brothel. You are. But continue on to the second floor and you will find one of Bumpattabumpah's most popular and stylish eateries. Specializing in Cambodian cuisine, Ho Binh is family run and your host Mr Chi has managed to put behind him his years of service as a Khmer Rouge information officer although beneath the convivial charm there lurks quite a temper and on no account should his recommendations be ignored.

Traveller's Tip Many Bumpattabumpah restaurants advertize live music, often in the form of a 'string quartet'. Be warned that this ensemble will traditionally consist of a banjo, two ukeleles and a yo-yo. 👍

Few diners fail to be impressed by the fine food and impeccable service at **Na Muang**, one of Bumpatta-bumpah's newest restaurants. Food here is prepared at your table in a flamboyant display of culinary skill and prices are quite reasonable although dry-cleaning costs will push the bill up a little. Elegant torches and candles make for a romantic atmosphere, the ambience shattered only by the regular sound of smoke alarms being set off.

✉ 75 Bump Sloh Duk Lu
☎ 33 653 922
▤ MC V

Jonathan Writes... *For the Luxury Traveller* Asking me to name my favourite restaurant in Bumpattabumpah is a little like asking me to write without pretentiously lapsing into French. *C'est impossible!* I am tempted, however, to give a *mention honorable* to the exquisite Yumbon where they serve a dessert of saffron-infused lime crab souffle with handmade Muscat-dipped peach sorbet towers. It's such a complicated dish that the kitchen require extra time to prepare, often about a week, but the wait is more than worth it. If I could be permitted one criticism, a small segment of vanilla pod was inadvertently left in my coulis. Hardly a sackable offence, although I do believe as a result of my complaint a pastry-chef was subsequently caned.

$$ Mid-Range

Over looking Sloh Duk Lake in the heart of Bumpatta-bumpah is the up-market (and therefore quite pricey) **Indochine 1**. But just a block back you'll find its sister restaurant, the less expensive **Indochine 2**. The food here is identical, in fact it's just left-overs scraped from the plates of diners at Indochine 1 earlier that day before being re-fried and served up as a buffet. Their signature dessert is pecan pie crumbs.

Indochine 1
✉ 235 Bump Sloh Duk Lu
Indochine 2
✉ 9 Thanon Pong

Set in a beautiful courtyard, the **Bhodi Tree** offers a quiet retreat from the hectic throng of downtown Bumpattabumpah, provided you're not seated too close to the karaoke bar. The restaurant specializes in fish and crab, all prepared in the local style (burnt to a crisp and drowned in chilli) and there's an extensive wine list offering 'French' vintages by the flagon or cask.

✉ 47 Thanon Klangpaan
☎ 33 792 528
▤ DC V
outdoor dining
live music

Philippe Writes... Most of the so-called 'local' cuisine restaurants serve anything but. Authentic Bumpattabumpahn food should have an astringent, sickly aftertaste but instead these wonderful dishes have drifted towards a tasty delicious variant. If you are enjoying the food in this region you shouldn't be! Shame!

✉ *22 Bump Sloh Duk Lu*
☎ *33 012 031*

Said to be one of the most romantic restaurants in Bumpattabumpah, the owners of **Sweethearts** proudly boast that 90% of couples dining here inevitably end up in bed – or at very least, a hospital stretcher.

✉ *152 Thanon Klangpaan*
  live music

Night-owls looking for a late evening drink and some cool jazz rhythms can't go past **Sinatras**, a sophisticated, downtown piano bar where resident crooner Buddy Kroona (or 'Ol' Four Eyes' as he's known to friends) delivers his own distinctive blend of east beats west standards like 'As Time Rows By' and 'The Lady is a Tran'.

Tina Writes... *For the Cautious Traveller*

Even in the most up-market restaurants pick-pockets and purse slashers are common. A standard ruse works like this. The 'waiter' will offer to take your coat or bag so he can 'hang it up' in the cloakroom. No sooner is the article out of sight than trained accomplices are going through the pockets and making off with any valuables. My solution is simple. Demand a table inside the cloakroom. That way you can enjoy a meal while keeping a constant eye on your possessions.

$ Inexpensive

✉ *231 Bump Sloh Duk Lu*
☎ *33 822 348*
▤ *MC V*

A small, laid-back eatery not far from the railway station, **Tubong Jyor** was closed last year for what the owners described as 'major renovations' during which time they appear to have mopped the floor. It's now open again for business serving a good range of rice dishes. ***Note*** *In our last edition we described much of the food here as 'oven-cooked'. This should, of course, have read 'over-cooked'.*

✉ *21 Thanon Klangpaan*
▤ *DC*

One of the great backpacker stand-bys, **The Ngoc Long** has very friendly staff and an ambitious menu; ask for anything and you'll hear confident replies of, 'Have. Have'. They haven't, but full marks for enthusiasm.

Somlor, a colonial-style restaurant, features cuisine ✉ *426 Suahu Nanlu*
from a by-gone era (before the advent of refrigeration or ☎ *33 122 701*
soap) and is popular with tourists staying at the nearby
hostel. The restaurant features nightly music and a
'cultural' dance show, inasmuch as two scantily clad
Thai strippers performing the 'Bustop' while lip-syncing
to Britney Spears can be described as cultural.

Sven Writes... *For the Budget Traveller*

It's a little known fact that the most expensive part of tom
yum soup is the prawns. Try ordering a serve without these
and you can be looking at a saving of up to 70%. Ask them
to hold the vegetables as well and you can be sitting down
to a steaming bowl of water and chilli powder for as little as
80p (US 8 cents).

DIANNE BREMENTON – FRIEND OF THE FISH

One of the most popular dishes in Southeast
Asia, and certainly Phaic Tan, is shark fin soup.
Considered cruel and unsustainable by many
wildlife protection agencies, sharks are caught
and 'finned', with the rest of their bodies – often
still alive – being dumped in the sea. One
Californian ex-pat animal rights activist, Dianne
Brementon, has recently started a **pilot program**
in which finless sharks are rescued and rehabilitated. At her private shark
sanctuary in Bumpattabumpah East Brementon painstakingly teaches de-
finned sharks to swim. The process is time-consuming and dangerous,
with on average one trainer a month losing a hand, but the work continues
and soon Dianne Brementon hopes to release her first 'graduates' back into
the ocean where they'll be allowed to swim free, thanks to prosthetic fins.
You can help this valuable work by refusing to order shark fin soup in any
Bumpattabumpah restaurants. Try one of the more acceptable alternatives,
such as *pho-mpho* (bear claw broth).

Bumpattabumpah After Dark

In addition to its many fine restaurants and cafes, Bumpattabumpah also boasts an exciting nightclub scene that continues to thrive despite the local population's tendency to go to bed around 7.30pm, coupled with the fact that its famous Floating Casino is now a dive site. For a nation so uniformly tone-deaf, karaoke remains a hugely popular entertainment option, as do bars and discos. Some of the more popular options are:

C Club Featuring a resident DJ (he's actually under house arrest) this funky hangout is popular with ex-pats looking for a fight.

Chasers features a Taiwanese blues band nightly, so it's rarely crowded, and you can sit at the bar or in the attached beer garden. Happy Hour is 9 to 9.05pm week nights. A big screen television shows a range of sporting events although many of these appear to be darts and snooker games from the late 1980s.

Built in typical Bumpattabumpah style (i.e. as a concealed arsenal), **Thuy Trla** is a good place to enjoy a few cocktails in a stylish, laid back setting. Very popular with the gay community, the club features a discrete – if somewhat ironic – rear entrance.

Those in search of something a little more sophisticated should visit the **Imperial Lounge**, an up-market cigar bar with stunning views out over the River Pong. Every night there's jazz with a local feel – the musicians don't bother tuning up – and it's the perfect place to enjoy a few single malts.

One of Bumpattabumpah's popular smoke-free nightclubs where complimentary cigarettes are offered to all customers.

From the outside **Pinky's** looks like a cheap and sleazy girlie bar, in fact it is, but downstairs you'll find a really cool saloon featuring a range of imported beers on tap. There's also a pool table but whenever an erotic floor show is underway upstairs the balls often go missing. There's also a decent sized dance floor featuring good music and a massive video screen that plays security camera footage of the previous week's armed hold-up attempts.

Opened to great fanfare in 2002, **Bong Bang** boasts a large dance floor lit by a series of faulty fluorescent globes, described by the owners as a 'state of the art' light show. There's no cover charge or, for that matter, fire exits.

Attractions

For most visitors to Bumpattabumpah **the Royal Palace** is the first stop on their sightseeing agenda. Built in 1680 by His Majesty King Tralahk IV, the Palace is a stunning example of 17th century Phaic Tanese architecture, featuring ebony walls, marble colonnades and a stunning Thai-style temple roof made up of genuine gold-plated tiles. It was the official residence of the Phaic Tanese Royal Family until 1956 when King Nhounchuc decided to move out after receiving a quote to re-tile the roof.

Note Very strict dress codes apply when visiting the Royal Palace, especially if the King is in residence. Men are expected to wear long trousers, shoes and a jacket. For women, His Majesty encourages halter tops and very short skirts. There is half-price admission for anyone in a bikini.

In 1995 the current King commissioned a life-sized **bronze statue** of his wife to grace the Palace courtyard. The first problem was the huge amount of bronze required – several tonnes had to be imported from China. Then, when completed, the weight of the piece caused the courtyard paving stones to buckle and collapse. The statue now leans at a sharp angle – as does Her Majesty – and provides welcome shade for visitors to the Palace grounds.

Traveller's Tip

Those planning a visit to any of Bumpattabumpah's many historical attractions should consider employing the services of a professional guide. Very few of them speak English but their knowledge of foreign currency exchange rates is generally excellent.

Sven Writes...
For the Budget Traveller

Museums and larger temples often charge hefty entrance fees, but if you turn up 15 minutes before closing time they'll generally let you in without charge. While you may not get to enjoy the complete cultural experience running from exhibit to exhibit, this is more than compensated for by the fact you'll have saved up to 50p (US 17 cents).

The **Phaic Tan Museum of History** opened just few years ago and is the country's attempt to chronicle 6000 years of human settlement, from its beginnings as a Neolithic village to its development as a trading village and finally its transformation into a modern nation state. An ambitious undertaking, given there are only two rooms (and one of these is the canteen) but it's well worth the visit. Look out for their excellent display of 20th century souvenir spoons and snow domes.

In the centre of town surrounding Sloh Duk lake are the **Ngoc Gardens**, regarded by locals as one of the city's beauty spots. Foreign visitors are more inclined to see them as a poorly drained, foul smelling bog but the gardens remain popular with joggers, cyclists and especially wedding parties, many of whom flock here on weekends. With so many people packed into such little space things can often turn violent and it's not unusual for couples, having exchanged vows, to then exchange fire with neighbouring parties.

At the northern end of the gardens you'll find a magnificent marble statue featuring **Ulqana**, the much-loved goddess of fertility (right). Extremely life-like, this statue is often visited by local couples hoping for children as well as by single men who like looking at breasts.

Wat Duop Prarm, also known as the Temple of the Wobbling Buddha, is the oldest and largest temple in Bumpattabumpah. Originally built as a place of religious learning Wat Duop gained notoriety a few years back when it became the first Buddhist University in the region to offer basketball scholarships. Most people go straight for the enormous statue in the southern section. It's more than 22 metres high and encrusted in a combination of gold leaf and pigeon poo inlaid with auspicious inscriptions. Behind the statue is a line of 61 bronze bowls, each representing a *laksana* ('characteristic') of the Buddha except for the last bowl, which is in fact an ashtray. Outside in the temple grounds are numerous sacred sites, including *chedis* (pavilions), *bots* (shrines) and the *irriwahti* (taxi rank).

Pokram Wat The people of Phaic Tan have a long history of mythical beasts and many of these feature at this magnificent temple complex. Above the gates you will see 10 *gharuas* (half-man, half-bird) while further inside the courtyard there is a large statue of an *aruhuya* (half-child, half-elf). If you'd like to see a *depaki* (half-woman, half-demon), there's one working in the tourist information booth. One of Bumpattabumpah's busiest temples, visitors can stop by at 5.30pm for evening prayers when the monks chant in harmony. Or come at 8.00pm for Happy Hour when they get quite raucous.

Considered by many to be one of the great icons of Bumpattabumpah, the **Royal Statue** sits grandly opposite Puppet Government House in Nu Soi square. Commissioned by King Pon Top in 1758 it was intended to celebrate his victory in the bloody battle of Thon Krep. The massive bronze statue was unveiled in 1761 and torn down the following day after his Majesty took offence at the lack of a bulge in the Regal Pants department. After the King's death this magnificent work of art was taken out of storage and re-installed as a proud symbol of the city's royal past. The statue itself, weighing over 15 tonnes, was long rumoured to be made of solid gold, a fact proved in 1985 when a portion of its head was removed and melted down to help fund Phaic Tan's bid to host the Southeast Asian Games.

RIGHT ROYAL GUARDS
Outside the Royal Palace you will see numerous colourfully dressed soldiers on duty, members of the King's own Royal Guard. Their uniform has actually undergone several modifications over the years. For a start, they now wear pants and their epaulettes have been reduced in size after high winds caused several commanding officers to become air-borne. Famous for their distinctive, high stepping march, the Royal Guards were forced to shorten stride some years back after members were continually knocking their own helmets off.

Phaic Tanese sandstone is widely used by local sculptors but unfortunately does not handle the elements well. This work, Infinity, *is barely three months old.*

Golf is starting to boom in Phaic Tan, however the **Royal Golf Club** in Bumpattabumpah remains the most famous. Originally designed by Jack Nicklaus and then re-modelled by a feng shui expert, it has many beautiful holes as well as some mystifying ones.

Always lush and green, it was built on some of the most fertile soil in the world. The grass grows so quickly here that the golf carts are in fact sit-on lawn mowers.

The wealth of the club's members is conspicuous. One will find it difficult to get a game unless you know someone in the military, the Royal family or the C.I.A.

The score-card shows the unorthodox hole numbers. These were chosen because they're deemed lucky. If you do indeed have a hole-in-one the club will mount and frame your golf cart.

Royal Phaic Tan Golf Club

NET SCORE

Player .... Handicap ....

Partner .... Handicap ....

C.C.R.

Date .... Home Club ....

Competition .... BLACK P.T.C.R. 76   BLUE A.C.R. 72

Hole	Metres	Metres	Par	Strokes Taken (Match/Index)	Player	+/-/o	Marker	+/-/o	Hole	Metres	Metres	Par	Strokes Taken (Match/Index)	Player	+/-/o	Marker	+/-/o
1	493	469	5	18	18				31	539	490	5	5	15			
+T 4	395	348	4	8	6				+G 43	164	162	3	11	8			
5	171	170	3	12	14				64	394	359	4	2	3			
6	418	389	4	3	4				65	284	273	4	15	17			
+T 9	340	325	4	14	12				+G 71	165	153	3	7	9			
22	370	357	4	6	10				73	359	335	4	13	11			
23	527	497	5	10	16				+G 90	387	339	4	4	7			
26	416	385	4	1	2				94	489	457	5	17	13			
+T 28	197	179	3	16	5				95	448	410	4	9	1			
OUT	3327	3119	36						IN	3229	2978	36					
									OUT	3329	3101	36					
									TOTAL	6558	6079	72					

MARKER ....

PLAYER ....

Medical Alert System   +T = Tec   +G = Green

Less Handicap

NET TOTAL

Designed by feng shui experts who sadly had little concept of public liability insurance. Players need to be exceptionally careful. The road toll from golf cart accidents continues to rise.

Special Conditions

(To be read in conjunction with the rules of golf)

1. **Galleries** For an extra fee the club can arrange to have a small gallery follow you around and applaud at appropriate intervals.

2. **Caddies** If caught in an electrical storm do not stand near trees or caddies. All caddies carry lightning rods and will bear the brunt of lightning strikes on your behalf.

3. **Water Hazards** All water hazards are defined by yellow stakes and contain scuba divers to retrieve your ball. They will surface and throw it closer to the pin without you incurring a penalty.

4. **Out of Bounds** The professional has declared his two very attractive daughters out of bounds to young members and guests. Infraction incurs great wrath and possibly one shot to the head penalty.

5. **Local Rule** Holes 5 & 6 are considered holy. You may still play them but you must take off your shoes and refrain from birdies out of respect.

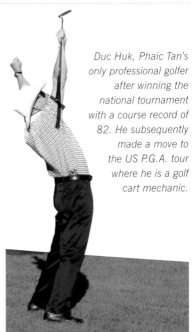

Duc Huk, Phaic Tan's only professional golfer after winning the national tournament with a course record of 82. He subsequently made a move to the US P.G.A. tour where he is a golf cart mechanic.

Bumpattabumpah's Floating Casino (below), taken shortly before the 2001 monsoon season. The casino still operates but now as a dive site, open to anyone with basic scuba skills. Unlucky underwater patrons have been known to re-surface, not only with the bends, but in debt.

Canals have always formed a major part of Bumpattabumpahn life and just about anywhere in the city can be reached quickly by local boatmen, adept at negotiating the narrow, interlaced waterways. So skilled are these oarsmen that in 1999 a squad of Phaic Tanese rowers came very close to qualifying for the Sydney Olympics, only missing out on selection when they stopped short of the finishing line to trade vegetables with the South Korean team.

When not cordoned off by riot police, the **Houses of Parliament** are well worth a visit. Check out the imposing portrait gallery featuring a painting of every Phaic Tanese Prime Minister along with the date on which he was assassinated.

A wonderful way to explore old Bumpattabumpah is via the many rivers and canals that wind their way through the city. Take a ***klongpong*** (flat-bottomed boat) driven by an authentically dressed ***klongnom*** (flat-bottomed boatman) for an intimate glimpse of traditional Phaic Tanese life. You'll see people using the various waterways to bathe, wash their clothes, cool off and even go to the toilet – although this last practice is technically banned within 100m of the Bumpattabumpah bottled water plant.

If you travel a short distance upstream along the **River Pong** you'll come to a 10ha island on which a replica of an historical village has been built. It's an authentic recreation of a traditional Phaic Tan community, set up to showcase the cultural and agricultural richness of the country. The exhibit had to be closed down a few years back when one group of pretend villagers set fire to crops belonging to others and full scale war broke out but the centre has now been re-opened with heavily armed 'peace keepers' patrolling regularly. You can witness and learn about local trades such as boat building, pottery making, weaving and prostitution.

Another must-see attraction on the River Pong is the city's famous **Floating Market**, where everything is traded, from fruit and veggies to handicrafts and political prisoners. One of the most fascinating parts of the floating market is its financial section, the Floating Stock Market, where slick young brokers in trendy canoes buy and sell shares. As a point of interest, Bumpattabumpah's stock exchange is the only one in the world to close for high tides.

(Opposite) The canals around Bumpattabumpah's floating market can get rather crowded, especially during clearance sales.

Bumpa-ttabumpah

Tina Writes...
For the Cautious Traveller
With droves of tourists wandering carelessly around, Bumpattabumpah is notorious for petty crime, particularly the motorbike 'snatch and run' variety. With an accomplice on the back, perps cruise the streets and grab bags from unsuspecting pedestrians. Which is why I always wrap my cash, credit cards and camera in condoms and swallow them before leaving the hotel.

Completed shortly after his death in 1947, the **Tomb of Chau Quoc** is a massive, square, forbidding structure overlooking the Royal Palace. Said to be modeled closely on Lenin's Mausoleum in Moscow, there's also a touch of Gracelands about this mammoth shrine where the revered leader of Phaic Tan's resistance movement lies in state, dressed in his trademark jewel-studded white jump-suit. Due to internal party wrangling the process of embalming Quoc's body did not actually commence until six weeks after he died, during which period the corpse was stored in less than perfect conditions. As a result the mummified figure is not in wonderful shape and, although discrete lighting helps soften the visual impact, it is not recommended for viewing by children.

From anywhere in Bumpattabumpah it's hard to avoid seeing the **Chuloc Towers**, a massive high-rise edifice that dominates the city skyline. Easily the tallest building in Phaic Tan, the Chuloc Towers were completed over a decade ago but, due to lack of demand, still remain largely empty. On the 75th floor there is an Observation Deck which is popular with visitors as well as investors in the project looking for somewhere to jump off.

MONEY TO BURN...

Throughout Bumpattabumpah visitors are likely come across the name Chu Umphang, generally regarded as one of the richest men in Phaic Tan. Born in Bumpattabumpah in 1933, Umphang made his fortune as the inventor of mono-sodium glutamate (or MSG), the flavour enhancer routinely added to just about all food in the region. Stories of this billionaire's big spending are quite legendary. In 1972 he flew over 300 guests to a castle in Scotland for his daughter's wedding. Some years later when his second daughter married he went one step further and flew the castle to Phaic Tan, stone by stone. A man of enormous appetite and ego, Umphang died in 1981 due to complications arising from penile enlargement surgery. (The donor rhino also passed away.)

The **Bumpattabumpah Botanical Gardens** (*right*) are well worth a visit as they feature one of the largest displays of vegetables in the world, divided into varieties that can be steamed, grilled or deep-fried. There's also a rice paddy and an extensive maze made up of bok choi. **Note** *To boost re-growth, curators use dung from specially bred diahhoretic elephants. Maps and guides are available at the entrance, as are gas-masks.*

Just across the road from the Chuloc Towers is a large building that houses the **Bumpattabumpah Craft Centre** where you can watch batik being made and view an audio visual presentation on the history, development and uses of batik. There's also a batik display, a hands-on workshop where you can make your own batik and every weekend they put on a fashion show featuring models dressed exclusively in batik. The Centre was opened by His Majesty in 1993. It is yet to have a visitor.

One of the city's newest family attractions, the **Nam Chak Water Slide Park and Elephant Sanctuary** offers a fun day out for those travelling with kids. The elephant shows are great fun (for the audience – the elephants themselves appear to be in some degree of pain); however, a visit to the Water Slide section is strongly advised against as several of the rides significantly exceed civil engineering safety standards dealing with velocity, vertical drop limits and exposed rivets. If you do choose to brave the park, on all accounts avoid riding the *Hhoc Whoa* ('the Big Enema').

Elephants at Nam Chak Park still perform shows despite many suffering from a rare form of eczema.

Traveller's Tip

The best way to learn about Bumpattabumpah's many historic sites is to take a guided tour. These can generally be booked and paid for as part of your entrance fee. Sometimes opportunistic visitors will attempt to 'attach' themselves to these group tours by following a short distance behind and 'eavesdropping' on the commentary. Be warned. Plain-clothed assistants carry bamboo poles (or *thwaks*) and non-paying visitors caught listening in can expect a severe thwacking.

Phaic Tanese Botany

Due to fertile soils, consistent rainfall and lax regulations covering genetic modifications, Phaic Tanese botanists have made grafting an art-form, introducing dozens of new hybrid plant species to the world. Amongst the more notable vegetative variants are:

Chinese Brocconvillea	Cherranium	Split Peatunia
Bok Chulip	Kiwisteria	Zucchivy
Tofuschia	Garlicalyptus	Pumpkinvillea
Orchidney Beans	Gingeranium	Watercressanthemum
Chickoranda Tree	Mangolia	Cyclamelon
Capsicumelia	Bananadendron	Dehydrangea

Bananadendron

Capsicumelia

Cherranium

Cyclamelon

Dehydrangea

Garlicalyptus

Other plant combinations are currently being worked on, with the hope of creating new botanical breakthroughs. Planned pairings include:

Beans + Artichokes = **Fartichokes**

Daffodil + Cannabis = **Spliffodil**

Nicotine + Fragrant Flowers = **Fagnolia**

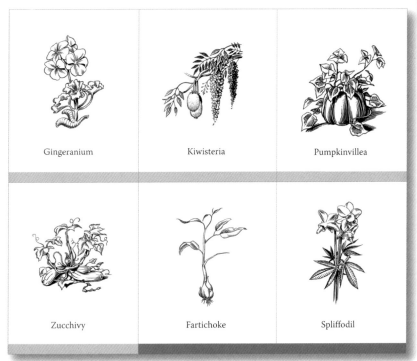

Gingeranium

Kiwisteria

Pumpkinvillea

Zucchivy

Fartichoke

Spliffodil

PLANNED PAIRINGS

HEALTH ALERT Due to the skill and dedication of many Bumpattabumpah bar girls, performances can often involve projectiles moving at high speed across the room. Patrons are advised, in addition to the standard safe sex precautions, to consider wearing protective eye goggles, especially if seated close to the bar.

Note Most bars and nightclubs in Bumpattabumpah's red light district close for major Buddhist holidays. In those that do stay open on these holy days the ladies may insist on dancing partially clothed.

Sex in the City

For many people Bumpattabumpah after dark is a city synonymous with sleaze, a place where cheap 'girlie bars' and recently de-registered temples offer a range of **exotic adult entertainment**. The truth is, Bumpattabumpah's notorious red light district is limited to just a few city blocks centred round the suburbs of **Dud Bhonk**, **Qic Phuk** and **Phlat Tiht**. Here, dimly lit bars featuring erotic dance shows sit side by side with Bumpattabumpahn Sex shops selling everything from **bamboo marital aids** to edible sarongs.

A Note of Caution

It goes without saying that most of the ladies working in Bumpattabumpah's seedier bars are available for a price and many western visitors do avail themselves of the opportunity to 'borrow' a companion for the evening.

Health Warning. If you do choose to patronize commercial sex workers in Bumpattabumpah, take **proper precautions** and use a latex condom. The locally made brands, whilst cheaper, cannot be relied upon due to inferior production standards and the fact they're made out of **rice paper.**

Professional Women

The Phaic Tanese actually have a long history of **hostesses** or 'wambhams',* women traditionally employed to help out in palaces and wealthy homes. An important distinction needs to be made between wambhams and modern sex workers. Wambhams are women schooled in the ancient art of hospitality and **courtly ritual**. These women are not prostitutes and will not provide sexual services, unless of course you pay them.

* *From the ancient Phaic Tanese Wambham Tankumam.*

Traveller's Tip

When staying at a hostel in the seedier sections of Bumpattabumpah, do not ask for a 'top bunk' unless you are after a prostitute wearing very high heels.

Phaic Tanese 'good time girls' will often wait for customers outside Bumpatta-bumpah's many inner-city bars.

Philippe Writes...

Not only do I find prostitution morally repugnant and offensive to women, it's also completely unnecessary. I've always found the bar girls of Bumpattabumpah surprisingly friendly. On a recent visit I got talking to one young waitress who obviously enjoyed my company so much she insisted on coming back to the hotel for, let's just say, 'a nightcap'. Despite the language barrier we really connected and I was saddened to see Sindy leave the next morning, but I didn't have time worry because, as it happened, my credit card and wallet had somehow gone missing and I needed to file a report.

03

Phaic Tăn
Thong On

Introduction

Situated in the country's far West, the **exotic**, coastal province of Thong On has long been a magnet for those wanting relief from the hustle and bustle of Phaic Tan's bigger cities. Here one can settle back in a lazy deck chair under a shady coconut palm and, on any given day, soak in the sight of an overloaded passenger ferry slowly sinking in the glittering azure sea. Or take a dawn climb to the summit of Mt Siyuden, an **extinct volcano** where the famed mystic Swami Ghit was said to have spent 14 years meditating in the lotus position under a boddhi tree before eventually having to be stretchered down with **severe cramp**.

If one word could be used to describe Thong On it would have to be 'lush'. The fertile volcanic soil, high humidity and almost constant rainfall create ideal growing conditions for everything from rice to tinea, with locals producing at least seven crops a year.

Thong On's extensive 'Mildew Coast' threads its way along 400km of rocky headlands, mountainous promontories, muddy deltas and untouched swamps. The actual amount of sandy beach is limited to just under 3km but this hasn't stopped many **vibrant tourist centres** springing up throughout the region. The capital Pattaponga attracts many families as well as mosquitoes while the many **islands** off shore are a haven for international visitors seeking a slice of 'tropical paradise'. Of course, human settlement in the area dates back many thousands of years. Well before tourists ever discovered Thong On, it is claimed that the Buddha himself came here to sit and contemplate on the beach. Local legend has it that this was the only time the Holy One ever had his hair braided.

Sadly, the region's popularity has seen enormous strains placed on it and there are areas that have not survived the tourist onslaught. Off shore, for example, the reef is in pretty poor shape with many sections bleached white due to pollution and **agricultural run-off**. However, moves are underway to repair the damage and much of the coral is now regularly painted. Over-development, too, has been a problem with **rampant construction** marring much of the coastal beauty. A statute prohibiting the erection of buildings taller than palm trees has had little effect, with developers simply importing **genetically modified trees** from Brazil, capable of growing up to 70 metres.

Traveller's Tip A good sarong is a must when visiting Thong On's more remote islands as it easily doubles as a beach blanket, towel, bed sheet, sun shield and bandage for head wounds.

When to Go

The west coast of Phaic Tan has two distinct weather periods: the Rainy Season and the Wet Season. The **best time to visit** is probably between these two seasons in May–August when strong monsoon winds lash the coast. While these winds may slightly hamper beach activities they do at least they keep the **sand flies** at bay.

Thong On has not suffered as greatly from land mines as other parts of the country and relatively few sections of the province are considered unsafe. Where UXO do exist the local government is undertaking extensive de-mining projects in which the unexploded ordinance is located, dug up and sold to North Korea.

If possible, time your trip to coincide with the full moon of each month, when local shop owners throughout the province turn off the electricity and hang **lanterns** bearing their shop's name. Hundreds of people are drawn out to celebrate on these nights, including shoppers, revelers and **professional thieves** keen to take advantage of non-functioning security alarms.

DIVING DAREDEVIL

One of the first foreigners to make his mark in Thong On was American-born Mike Gainsman who moved here during the 1960s. Something of a thrill-seeker, Mike became intrigued by the possibility of attempting a dive off the rugged Pattaponga cliff-top north of the town – a feat many locals declared impossible due to the shallow water. But after months of careful observation, Mike noted that the spring tides came in sets of seven, the last wave of which giving an average depth of 12m. On June 20, 1967, in front of a crowd of almost 1000, he executed a perfect swan dive. The only thing Mike failed to take into account was the fact he couldn't swim and was subsequently drowned. A plaque now marks the spot where his body was washed ashore.

BATHERS BEWARE!

Even though it may be acceptable in your own country, remember that the sight of nude or partially nude bathers is considered deeply offensive to the Phaic Tanese and many local men will travel dozens of miles just to remind themselves of the fact.

History

The administrative capital of Thong On province is Pattaponga, a **sprawling coastal centre** that began life several hundred years ago as a sleepy fishing village. These days the only reminder of this **piscatorial past** is the lingering aroma and a few wizened old salts eyeing the horizon and waiting patiently for trucks to bring in a load of frozen seafood from distant ports. Pattaponga first became famous as a **Royal holiday retreat** in the 16th century after the Queen visited and spoke of a vision in which she was impregnated by an elephant. Court astrologers described this dream as extremely auspicious (the Queen described it as a nightmare) and decreed that a holiday palace be built on the spot.

Around 1640, both the Dutch and Portuguese landed near Pattaponga and proceeded to fight over ownership of the coastal strip, both insisting that the other should have it. This dispute, known as '**The War of Polite Insistence**', raged for almost a decade before France stepped in and claimed the entire region. By this stage the locals were wary of European settlers and initially refused to allow any to settle in their land. In 1729 the French sent an envoy, Jules LeFreq, to discuss a **treaty**. He was greeted warmly – in fact he was roasted over hot coals – and war was declared. In February the following year 20,000 French troops armed with canon, rifles, bayonets and swords invaded. They were met by a platoon of local militia armed with masks depicting fearsome evil spirits. The resulting **massacre** was horrific and the French invaders had little trouble taking over the city.

Under their control Pattaponga expanded rapidly and, while sanitation and poverty remained a constant problem, over 500 bakeries soon sprang up. The French soon began using Pattaponga as a **trading post**, exporting rice, spices and – for a short time – slaves. Unfortunately for the French, Pattapongan slaves soon developed a reputation for being particularly strong-willed and militant; several shiploads were sent back by one disgruntled buyer after they began demanding overtime and a holiday pay loading.

Like most Phaic Tanese cities, Pattaponga fought a long and bloody battle for **independence**, led by communist rebel leader Colonel Kru Kut (1881– 38). A man of many contradictions, Kru Kut believed fervently in the right of all men to live free from tyranny yet would regularly beat to death the men responsible for cleaning his pool. On the evening of June 28, 1913, Kru Kut led an **uprising** that saw the government garrison stormed. 750 French soldiers were killed, many of them seriously, and the city was at last free from colonial rule. Kru Kut was appointed Governor and went on to hold numerous other posts including Mayor, Chief Magistrate and **Bachelor of the Year** before his death in 1938 when a 21-gun salute went horribly wrong.

Pattaponga

For many visitors Pattaponga is merely a stepping off point for trips along the west coast or to its out-lying islands but the truth is this **vibrant city** has much to offer in its own right – the Old City, for example, where traffic is banned and you can wander through a maze of **ancient temples** and shops. Of course, the original opium dens and brothels have long since been closed down (you'll now find them in the diplomatic quarter), but a few hours here still provide a unique glimpse back to a time before tourism or **surveillance cameras**.

Remember too that Pattaponga is home to the region's only hospital, the Bansak Memorial. This **world-class facility** made the headlines a few years back when, several months after being discharged, a patient discovered a pair of surgical scissors had been left in her abdomen. Doctors were understandably embarrassed and somewhat baffled as the woman had only been treated for a middle ear infection.

The Bansak Hospital casualty ward can get pretty crowded, especially during holiday season, and in an effort to spread the load medical staff have introduced a 'happy hour'. Get your foot stitched or stomach pumped (between 5 and 6pm) for half price.

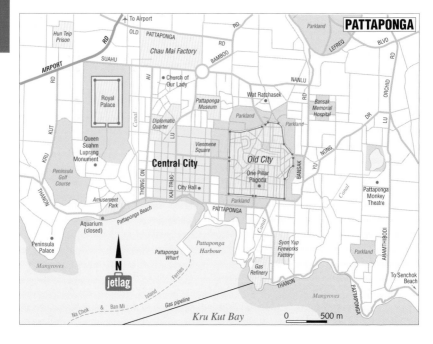

Then there's Pattaponga's world famous beach, a stunning 500m sweep of **coarse brown sand** ringed by majestic mangroves and ice-cream vans. It was here in the late 70s that a young David Bowie walked barefoot through the shallows and trod on a **stonefish**. Nowadays surfers come here from all over the world, drawn by the notorious 'Pattaponga Break' where huge waves are created by strong **ocean currents** hitting the off shore gas pipeline. The beach itself is lined with stores selling T-shirts and cold drinks, **laid-back cafes** and thin local villagers renting themselves out as surfboards. The waves that make Pattaponga such a great beach for surfers make it less suitable for swimming, with a strong undertow and numerous **rips**. Lifeguards are stationed in special towers all along the beach although due to a **design flaw** few of these towers actually have a view of the water so you're pretty much on your own. Note that during the **monsoon season** the currents along Pattaponga beach are particularly strong and it is not recommended for swimming unless you are extremely competent or have an interest in visiting the Cape of Good Hope.

Though crowded with sun-lovers during the day, the beach remains amazingly clean and also refreshingly clear of **hawkers**, thanks to local by-laws making it an offence to possess hair-beading accessories without a license. There are, however, a multitude of beggars to be found, spread along the beach with their hands pleadingly outstretched – hence the frequent reference to this 'palm-lined coast'. Of course, a stroll along the foreshore first thing in the morning reveals a whole new world, as **local fishermen** in their brightly coloured boats patrol the bountiful shallows. These men still use traditional methods – dynamite – and come ashore each day around dawn to sort through their catch that includes everything from fish and prawns to squid and **semi-conscious scuba divers**.

Enterprising locals in Pattaponga benefit from the sinking of a cargo freighter carrying a shipment of teak furniture.

Getting There

Even though it's a relatively short distance from the capital Bumpattabumpah, the easiest way to reach Pattaponga is by air. Roads into the region are narrow and often blocked by mudslides and those choosing to come by **rental car** will have to pay, not only for the vehicle, but an additional fee for every stray dog or backpacker run over on the trip. Bus trips are cheaper but seem to take forever, especially when drivers will generally insist on halting at the outskirts of the city to allow the on-board video to finish.

Phaic Tan's regional airline, Southeast Asia Royal Service (SARS), makes regular trips into Pattaponga and **ticket prices** are low. SARS boasts one of the oldest passenger airline fleets in the world and very few of their aircraft are I.F.R. (instrument flight rules) rated, meaning that pilots must rely on visual flying techniques, a slight worry as so many of them are short-sighted. As with many regional airlines, SARS flights will not take off until the plane is full and at least one passenger must volunteer to help manually **retract the landing gear**.

__Warning__ The X-ray machines at Pattaponga Airport are notorious for being turned up high and there's a fair chance that unexposed film may be ruined. On the up-side, security staff monitoring the machines will let passengers know if they require dental fillings.

At the airport you'll be confronted by a barrage of 'transport touts' in a variety of vehicles, all offering cheap rides into town, and choosing one can be somewhat overwhelming. Look out for the blue cars with the word Tahxi emblazoned on the side. These are not cabs – the word 'tahxi' is local slang for 'impounded or stolen vehicle'. Of course, if you've booked into a hotel and pre-paid for a **transfer service** then head out to the front of the terminal. You're unlikely to find a shuttle but there are public phones available to register a complaint.

Sven Writes...
For the Budget Traveller

A good way to cut down on transport costs is to hire a cyclo and then offer to help peddle in return for 20% off the fare.

Getting Around

With its crowded, chaotic streets and heavy traffic the best way to get around the city is on board a *tuktuk*, a motorised three-wheel rickshaw or a *phukttuk*, a de-commissioned *tuk tuk* without brakes. Whether you take private or public transport, expect traffic jams during the morning rush between 6 and 9am and again between 4 and 7pm. For the rest of the day it's gridlock.

Dulaks, *often referred to as the 'Gondoliers of the East', resent comparisons to their Venetian counterparts. However, for some reason they do speak Italian.*

Where to Stay

Pattaponga offers a good range of accommodation options, both in town and along the waterfront. Many of these places now boast their own website although visitors making advanced on-line bookings should be warned that in many cases the photos used bear little or no relationship to the actual hotel. It's also worth noting that in Pattaponga the terms 'villa', 'condominium', 'chateau' and 'resort' are used are used to refer to any building structure not made of plywood.

$$$ Expensive

✉ *43 Suahu Nanlu*
☎ *39 852 221*
@ *chiva@phoni.com.pt*
▤ *DC MC V*

Viong Truohm Resort If you're looking for the ultimate in luxury, go no further than this grand complex on the main beach just south of town. A dozen private bungalows sit in landscaped grounds enjoying views out over the ocean. The lawns are manicured – literally – by ground staff armed with small scissors and a nail file who patrol the grassy expanses on their knees. The emphasis here is on total relaxation – guests checking in are offered a complimentary neck and shoulder massage, rooms are serviced hourly and there's a free stretch shuttle limo service into town.

✉ *89 Thanon Pattaponga*
☎ *39 192 455*
@ *www.girls.com.pt*
▤ *DC MC*
  topless check-in
  pool
  gym

The Beachside Inn This resort boasts the largest pool in the country, complete with slides, its own beach and – according to several witnesses – a school of reef sharks. For gym junkies, the Beachside currently has a massive health and fitness club under construction; guests seeking a serious work-out are welcome to sign on as labourers.

✉ *263 Ahamthibodi Lu*
☎ *39 884 239*
@ *pal@phoni.com.pt*
▤ *MC*
  golf course with
  fully stocked bar

The city's oldest luxury hotel, the **Peninsula Palace** is part of the international Stanford chain, meaning that you can steal a bathrobe here and be arrested in any one of 27 other countries around the world. A large, well-run complex, the Peninsula is popular with golfers keen to play its championship course. Designed by US pro John Daly, it features ashtrays and a fully stocked bar at the start of each hole.

Warning *Golfers playing the Peninsula course should be reminded that many of the bunkers are heavily mined and players setting off an explosion will be penalized two strokes.*

The **Ocean Grand** was built on top of two blocks of pre-war shophouses, and hints of this colonial past can still be detected in the hotel's architecture, along with the faint cries of families living in underground air pockets. Despite its size, the Grand boasts a serene, tasteful atmosphere, and there are some unique features, like the lovingly restored iron elevator – a device so slow that guests traveling more than three floors may require a late check out. One minor criticism is that the hotel backs onto an extremely busy thoroughfare, although limo drivers entering or leaving the Grand are assisted by uniformed staff who will fling themselves onto the road as human speed humps to slow on-coming traffic.

✉ *132 Thanon Pattaponga*
☎ *39 990 266*
@ *grand@phalti.com.pt*
▤ *DC MC V*

Shangri-La Inn One of the city's newer hotels (it was built in 1962), the Shangri-La boasts a staggering array of guest facilities. All the suites come with their own personal butler, complimentary cocktails and breakfast, all night pillow fluffing, free local calls, your own pants press, your own pants, daily newspaper delivery, someone to read it to you and a sunken bath so large it's possible to do laps. The hotel also offers free laundering of clothes or foreign currencies. Guest rooms also feature hand-woven carpets, each one with its own certificate of authenticity, featuring a photo of the pre-school child who made it. Those wanting to keep fit can choose between the gymnasium, squash courts or one of the hotel's two indoor, air-conditioned tennis courts, both staffed with a resident professional coach and ESPN commentary team standing by to call your match.

✉ *200 Ahamthibodi Lu*
☎ *39 376 886*
@ *shangi@phoni.com.pt*
www.shangi.com.pt
▤ *DC MC V*

Jonathan Writes... *For the Luxury Traveller*

When visiting Thong On I always stay at Shangri-La and the staff there know me well, not surprising really, as I've had many of them sacked for impertinence. What I particularly like about the Shang is that it's so self-contained; the resort is practically a city in itself, with shops, several restaurants, a medical clinic and even its own prison. The rooms are large and all have a distinctly European feel about them, so much so that you'd never know you were in Phaic Tan, if it weren't for the smell. C'est magnifique!

$$ Mid-Range

✉ *286 Thanon Pattaponga*
☎ *39 772 845*
🖮 *MC*
  live music

One of Pattaponga's original guesthouses, the **Surfside Hotel** was completely renovated in the late 90s. So extensive was this refurbishment that only the original front doors and some of the rat population remain. Popular with families on a budget, the Surfside offers basic, clean rooms most with their own bath although you may pay extra for a plug. A traditional folk band not only serenades visitors as they arrive, they also provide wake-up calls.

✉ *12 Suahu Nanlu*
☎ *39 656 223*
🖮 *MC V*

Situated on a rocky promontory north of town, the **Kim Sen Resort** is perfect for those wanting to get away from the hustle and bustle. You certainly won't be disturbed by room service or maintenance workers, as the Kim Sen features a somewhat minimalist approach to staffing levels. 'Ocean View' rooms look out to where the beach used to be before it was washed away by Cylone Hector III in 1996.

✉ *6843 Khai Truc Lu*

Three Seasons Hotel Another out-of-town option, the Three Season's location may not suit everyone but if interstate truck routes are your interest this friendly, reasonably priced hotel is perfect. All of the rooms feature subdued lighting, meaning you won't see the cigarette burns on the carpet, and TVs featuring Phaic Tan's popular Pirate Movie Channel. The hotel also boasts a 'Business Centre', although at the time of writing this appeared to consist of two chairs, a small desk and a broken stapler. When checking in ask about a non-smoking room. They don't have any but management is conducting a survey.

✉ *8359 Khai Truc Lu*
☎ *39 331 922*
🖮 *DC MC V*

The Royal Ocean View Luxury Palace Officially one of the top five Misleading Hotels of the World, the Ocean View is in fact some 15km inland. Built in the style of a traditional Phaic Tanese palace, the resort offers authentic architectural touches such as uneven floors and doors that don't quite shut. But the service is excellent with rooms cleaned daily and, as a lovely touch, a single lotus bloom left on your pillow will tell you that the maid has been through. That, and the fact your wallet will be missing.

$ Budget

Known as a surfie's hangout, the **Pipeline Hotel** takes its name, not from the rolling sets of waves on its nearby beach, but the large ocean outfall sewer that drains onto the sand opposite the guest cottages. Facilities are a little limited, with the hotel's two tennis courts currently closed for soy bean cultivation but there is a range of leisure activities on offer, including cooking lessons, fruit carving and visits to the hotel's very own insect museum (also known as the Guest Laundry).

⊠ *322 Thanon Pattaponga*
☏ *39 768 423*
▤ *DC MC*

Hau Pah Villas This basic hotel advertises itself as being 'a mere 50 metres from the beach' and, while this claim is technically true, it should be borne in mind that the trip involves crossing a multi-lane expressway. The hotel itself offers basic facilities and is popular with families who can enjoy its games room, playground and very own Underwater World, also known as the basement car park.

⊠ *327 Ahamthibodi Lu*
pool

The **Pattaponga Golden Beach Inn** is casual and comfortable, with a tropical open-air lobby to allow for cool breezes – very pleasant on a hot day although during hurricane season it may be necessary for guests to anchor themselves to the floor while checking in. Deluxe rooms have windows overlooking the parking area while in the cheaper Standard rooms the concept of windows appears to have been overlooked altogether. All upper-storey rooms are carpeted which, while lacking the tropical charm of timber flooring, does help to partially muffle the sound of the karaoke bar below.

⊠ *322 Suahu Nanlu*
☏ *39 472 955*
▤ *DC V*

Sea Breezes is a small and very quiet, bungalow-style resort popular with surfers and those on methadone programs. Rooms are small and fairly dim, in keeping with the staff, and the resort boasts a large pool designed to look like a natural pond; certainly the surface scum appears authentic.

⊠ *3443 Khai Truc Lu*
▤ *MC*
pool

Note *Despite Sea Breezes' claim to be 'just a short stroll' from the beach, this trip should only be undertaken by determined walkers with a high level of fitness and at least half a day to spare.*

Where to Eat

Despite being on the coast and boasting its own large fishing fleet, most seafood caught in Pattaponga is in fact packed on ice and exported to China or Japan. But some less sought-after produce is kept and, over the years, local chefs have come up with a range of inventive dishes such as prawn shell soup, crab claw salad and, a regional favourite, barbecued fish scales on a bed of sun-dried algae. Being a tourist town, there's a wide range of eating options, from authentic noodle bars and street stall vendors through to western-style steak and pizza joints. There was even a McDonalds planned a few years back but building work stalled when local feng shui experts placed the ordering booth 30m back from the driveway.

Note *When eating seafood in Pattaponga remember that looks can be deceiving. Local caviar is not, in fact, fish eggs but fish eyes. That said, it's still remarkably expensive.*

$$$ Expensive

⌧ *174 Thanon Pattaponga*
☏ *39 531 552*
▤ *DC MC V*
     live music

Keow Bhan Considered *the* place to eat in Pattaponga, Keow Bhan offers the ultimate in fine dining. Attentive service, beautiful table settings and stylish food, including the restaurant's signature dish, a local version of surf 'n' turf – shark 'n' bark. The wine list is so extensive that it comes in two volumes, A–K and L–Z. On Saturday and Sunday nights a local Dixieland jazz band plays so if you enjoy good music, consider booking a table mid-week.

⌧ *69 Ahamthibodi Lu*
☏ *39 232 953*
▤ *DC V*

La Marina Situated on a pier right out over the water you can sip cocktails here while watching unsuspecting windsurfers being swept out to sea. Fresh seafood is the specialty of La Marina and diners may select their meal from a large tank of live fish along one wall. Of course, meat eaters don't miss out either. A waiter will accompany you to a series of holding pens out the back where an impressive selection of livestock is caged. Just point to your selection and a sous chef armed with a baseball bat will do the rest.

Jonathan Writes... *For the Luxury Traveller* If you're dining out in Pattaponga you simply must try the local specialty *putra gulung*. An intensely rich dish, it involves a frog stuffed into a chicken which is in turn stuffed into a piglet stuffed into a sheep. The entire concoction is then slathered in butter and slow roasted before being stuffed into your mouth by a team of specially trained waiters. It's so filling I often don't need to eat again for at least an hour.

TJ's by the Sea If the beautiful ocean view and magnificent food don't make you want to swoon, the smell from the nearby tuna processing plant almost certainly will. Traditional touches, such as cracked crockery and wobbly tables, further enhance the atmosphere. Despite the elegant surrounds and excellent service, the food at TJ's is surprisingly good value. For under 2000p you can order the fisherman's basket. For another 2000p you can order some food to go in it. There's also a wine list so extensive it's unlikely that you'll stump the barman (unless you happen to ask for a clean glass).

✉ *37 Thanon Pattaponga*
☎ *39 765 234*
▤ *MC V*

Chez Hu Sophistication and style blend in this elegant French bistro just a few minutes from the centre of town. Dark ivory is widely featured throughout the restaurant, even in some of their desserts, and the lighting – by Phaic Tanese standards – is subdued, with just a few bare fluorescent strips dangling above each table. As its name implies, Chez Hu serves French fare but with a strange literal twist. (It's worth pointing out that their coq au vin does not involve chicken.) The owner Mr Hu greets diners at the front door, welcoming regulars and frisking new-comers with practised ease as he barks orders at his hard-working, indentured staff.

✉ *153 Suahu Nanlu*
☎ *39 060 442*
@ *www.chezhu.com.pt*
▤ *MC*

$$ Mid-Range

Abdun For a broad range sampling of Phaic Tanese cuisine, try Abdun, a buffet-style eatery in the centre of town. Prices here are set according to weight – diners step on a set of scales before and then after eating their meal, with the two figures used to tabulate a final cost. A good value, if mildly demeaning dining option.

✉ *75 Suahu Nanlu*
☎ *39 283 554*

Wah Nuri Despite being situated several hundred metres back from the beach, the place has a laid-back beachside feel and they still manage to get a lot of sand in the food. Everything here is open plan, including the kitchen and – somewhat disturbingly – the bathrooms.
Note *The large wine buckets on the tables are in fact cigar ashtrays.*

✉ *2646 Khai Truc Lu*
☎ *39 573 288*
▤ *DC V*

✉ *47 Ahamthibodi Lu*
outdoor dining

Café Karma Located in a new complex opposite the Town Hall, Café Karma features minimalist décor – there's just one table and no chairs – and a fairly limited menu. Your best option is to head for the courtyard dining area, a serene garden setting where diners can sip cocktails in the shade of lush stinging nettles.

Note *At night bats swoop to catch bugs, only themselves to be caught by kitchen staff and served up as the 'Chicken Surprise'.*

✉ *88 Suahu Nanlu*
☎ *39 533 112*
@ *hootaz@phoni.com.pt*
🗐 *DC MC V*

Hootaz Definitely one for adults only, this bawdy beer hall-cum-café is popular with bucks nights and large groups of revelers. The food is actually quite traditional and most of it comes wrapped in banana leaf, as do the waitresses. Weekends get pretty rowdy and around 10pm there's a 'Foxy Floorshow' that culminates in a scantily clad woman leaping out of a fishcake.

Sven Writes... *For the Budget Traveller* At many restaurants in Phaic Tan the waiter will bring you a hot towel at the start of the meal. I always carry a bar of soap and use the opportunity to head to the bathroom for a complete body wash, thus avoiding the expense of paying extra for a hotel room with a shower.

$ Inexpensive

✉ *9 Thanon Pattaponga*
vegetarian/road-kill
meals available

The Boddhi Tree Named after the tree under which the Buddha 'saw the light' this eco-friendly café is run by a Buddhist couple. Not surprisingly, the menu is mainly vegetarian (buddhists are not allowed to deliberately kill anything) although they will serve seafood found washed up on the beach, as well as road-kill. Breakfast is served all day, except at breakfast.

✉ *985 Khai Truc Lu*
☎ *39 583 166*
🗐 *DC MC V*

Fresh Start Café One of the newest restaurants in Pattaponga, this is an NGO (non-government organization) project where disadvantaged locals are given shelter and taught useful skills such as folding napkins and credit card skimming. Everyone from homeless youths to drug addicts are welcome to work here, naturally enough under strict supervision, and the actual food preparation is handled by qualified lepers.

Wat Nhot One of the most popular places in town, Wat Nhot is packed most nights of the week. This has little to do with the food, it's simply one of the few restaurants in town to have air-conditioning. A long list of fresh seafood is prepared as you like it, provided you like it over-cooked and drowned in peanut sauce.

✉ *175 Suahu Nanlu*
☎ *39 561 668*

Le Bistro Whilst a specialty of the house is brains, it's not a feature readily shared by the staff who struggle to get the simplest of orders right. Formerly a bank, Le Bistro still retains many features such as thick brick walls, dark interiors and regular armed hold-ups.

✉ *99b Ahamthibodi Lu*

For diners 'on the run', Pattaponga boasts several good bakeries where you can pop in for a quick bowl of fried noodles and a coffee. Or, for those in a real hurry, you can have fried noodles in your coffee as a take-away option. Another quick meal option making its way into the city are Juice Bars. Many of these places use large industrial juicing machines operated by under-trained staff – insist on asking to count your juice-maker's fingers before drinking.

Philippe Writes...

I'm always amused by tourists who go into a restaurant and insist on ordering the 'Set Menu', thinking it's easier than making individual selections. What they end up getting is a bland, sprinkling of local flavours, served up with no real thought or care. I make a point of selecting something that's not actually on the menu so that a staff member must go out and purchase it. While some waiters may appear mildly annoyed and even short-tempered, the fact is they respect my defined culinary tastes and look forward to serving me, so much so that I rarely feel the obligation to leave a tip. My presence is bonus enough.

Attractions

Pattaponga makes an ideal base from which to enjoy a range of exciting activities and attractions. In the heart of town you'll find unique shopping opportunities such as **Vienmienne Square**, an area famous for its hand-woven textiles. Silk made here is slightly coarser than Thai silk but still widely used in door mats and industrial carpeting. Visitors seeking an adrenaline rush need travel no further than the Pattaponga **Bungee Jumping Centre**, just twenty minutes from town by ambulance. And those wanting to escape the hustle of city living should remember that there are dozens of islands just off-shore, many of them uninhabited, and for just a few hundred p'ting local boatmen will drop you off there. Picking you up may require several thousand p'tang but a day on these idyllic rocky escarpments is well worth the ransom.

Pattaponga's central landmark, the **Royal Palace**, is an impressive if somewhat crumbling castle once used by the royal family as a holiday retreat. Designed and built entirely by local artisans during the 17th century, the Palace was always prone to flooding and has suffered greatly over the years from water damage. Paradoxically, the only part of the building to have always remained dry is its moat.

A flock of pigeons in Vienmienne Square spot someone approaching with a wok.

Outside the gates of the Palace you will see an imposing granite figure. In 1996 King Tralanhng commissioned sculptors from each province to come up with a work of art that would capture the beauty and grace of his wife, **Her Majesty Queen Suahm Luprang**. This massive bulbous stone block, covered in deep cracks and fissures, was deemed the winner by a team of judges whose bodies are now rumoured to be interred, along with that of the artist responsible, within its foundations.

Hun Teip Prison Built during the 1850s by French authorities to incarcerate local dissidents, this dark, dank underground cavern is a grim reminder of the stark conditions faced by political prisoners during their long struggle for independence. The prison is open for public viewing on Saturdays and Sundays only. Mid-week it is used as an international telephone call centre.

The Pattaponga Museum holds a good collection of exhibits, ranging from modern displays of technology such as the world's first nuclear powered air-conditioner through to primitive Neolithic stone implements on loan from the local hospital.

Sven Writes...
For the Budget Traveller

The Royal Palace would have to be one of the most popular attractions in Pattaponga and every day thousands of visitors come to see it. Of course, this means the queues can get pretty long but if you're prepared to get there early and wait a few hours you can then sell your place in the line to a wealthy American tourist for a handsome fee. You won't ever actually get to see one of the architectural marvels of Southeast Asia, but this fact is more than made up for by the money you'll make.

Pattapongan fortune tellers are highly skilled at predicting your future. For a reduced fee, some will also predict your past, describing in precise detail what happened yesterday.

Opposite the old city gates you'll find the site of Pattaponga's **One Pillar Pagoda**. Built entirely out of wood in 1145 this architectural marvel survived undamaged for almost half an hour before blowing over and shattering during a mild sea breeze. A small plaque now marks the site. Numerous other sculptures and works of religious art can be found nearby including an impressive wooden statue of Cuc Luh, the goddess of mercy, slaughtering her mother.

Possibly the city's most infamous landmark, the ancient **Chau Mai Distillery** makes a famous local brand of fish sauce. When the wind blows from the north the smell from this factory is so over-powering that it is argued by many historians to be the reason Pattaponga took so long to be invaded.

City Hall This grand edifice was built between 1870 and a brothel. Designed in classical French style, the municipal building is well preserved and looks pretty much the same as it did when it first opened, although since then some of the toilets have been cleaned. The marble archway and platform out front are still used for important civil proclamations such as royal deaths and late TV listing changes.

The **Pattaponga Monkey Theatre** (right) is just a short drive east of town and always a great hit with the kids. There are several shows a day during which the animals perform a range of tricks in silly costumes. It's good, lighthearted fun although there is a serious side to the troupe with word that they're currently working on a performance of *King Lear*.

Nathaniel Blake's House A New York businessman who settled in the coastal resort of Pattaponga shortly after World War II, Nathaniel Blake lived in this fortified compound with a retinue of wives, mistresses, concubines and comfort women. Oddly enough, he was gay.

Wat Ratchasek One of the city's most venerated shrines yet, oddly, the most delapidated, this Wat was built by **King Ramchap** in the 16th century. Architecturally the temple complex represents a microcosm of the world. The foundations are Earth, the square base symbolizes Man and the domed roof is to help pick up Sky Sports. Most visitors head straight for the **Golden Buddha** in the northern section. This mysterious statue features the Buddha with one hand pointing down and the other up, believed by many to signify a rejection of evil and calling to mother earth for wisdom. Others believe it is an early attempt at disco dancing. Whatever the case, the statue itself is a copy, the original solid gold version having been placed in a vault at the State Bank for safe keeping in 1958 where it remained for six weeks before being stolen by an assistant manager. At the opposite end of the Wat is a shrine featuring a series of murals depicting major events in the Buddha's life including his birth, enlightenment and **21st birthday party**.

The Church of Our Lady One of the few Christian churches to have survived the post colonial era, this magnificent building was designed by French architect Louis Beirmonde and completed in 1862. Above the front door of the main entrance you'll see a bronze-toned, cast iron statue of the church's first priest Monsignor LeVecelle fondling two altar boys. The church has undergone numerous alterations over the past century, with stain glass windows and a cupola added by Archbishop Kweon during the 1930s. The billiard room and barbecue area were added a few years later by his brother-in-law.

Out front of the Church is a small courtyard with a French colonial-era fountain featuring a statue of a cherubic boy. In recent years the water flow has been reduced to a trickle and plumbing experts have so far been unable to fix the problem. At the time of writing local authorities were thinking about consulting a urologist.

FIREWORKS FAME
The Syon Yup fireworks factory in downtown Pattaponga is famous for having caught fire more often than any other commercial building in the world. Since its grand, yet illegal, opening in 1982 the factory has been burnt to the ground on a total of 17 separate occasions, including most recently in 2003 when the building's newly installed sprinkler system mysteriously burst into flame. Fortunately, no one was killed as, at the time, the entire workforce was out the back having a smoke.

DON'T MISS
A caretaker at Wat Ratchasek will proudly tell you about the temple's magnificent prudi *resting on sculpted* myet *and guarded by a* wihoon *that runs from the* yuap *all the way down to the* prang*. He is quite mad and has no idea what any of this means.*

Tina Writes...
For the Cautious Traveller
Pickpockets and
petty thieves tend to
congregate in areas
frequented by tourists.
My tip is to avoid
sights of cultural
significance or
historical interest.

THE PEOPLE'S POET
Out the front of City Hall you'll
notice a large bronze statue of
Tioc Hin (1911–42), one of the
city's most famous romantic
poets. Born to a wealthy family
of merchants, Tioc Hin wrote
numerous sonnets and epic
odes about the power of love.
In 1932 the country went to war
and he was conscripted into the
army but refused to serve on
the grounds he was a pacifist,
saying 'Love is a more powerful
force'. When the draft board
disagreed Tioc Hin hacked the lot
of them to death with a machete.

On a somewhat less cultural note, the **Pattaponga
Amusement Park** is a great place to visit if you have
children and are not unduly concerned about their
safety. Popular rides include a dodgem-car street
circuit and a fast-spinning carousel made entirely
out of a disused Russian uranium processing
centrifuge. There's also a mini '**Seaworld**' in which
trained tuna fish leap acrobatically out of a pool
and into the arms of a sushi chef. One word of
warning. The park's '**House of Horrors**' is just
that – a dark building featuring graphic photos of
political prisoners being tortured and shot.

Sea Turtles
About an hour's drive south along the coast
from Pattaponga will bring you to world famous
Senchok Beach. It is here every spring that rare
leatherback turtles (*Dermochelys coriacea*) come
ashore to lay their eggs. So if you're in town during
May to June you might be lucky enough to catch
a glimpse of these majestic sea creatures as they
make their way up the beach and into the back of
a **refrigerated poacher's van**.

Beach Activities

It's true that Pattaponga Beach has suffered in recent years from the city's unregulated construction boom. There are now so many **high-rise buildings** along its once famous foreshore that large sections of the beach are left in **permanent shade**. In some places the sand actually has moss growing on it. But on the upside, you'll save money on sunscreen. Of course for many people visiting the city, the only activity they'll be interested in is lazing on this magnificent coastal strip under the shade of a **reinforced sandfly net**. But there is a range of exciting entertainment options.

Numerous operators offer **parasailing** trips, a great way to get a bird's-eye view of the coastline. One hour aloft can cost as little as 3000p although there is often an additional surcharge if you want to be lowered down. If speed's your thing, there are plenty of **jet skis** for rent along Pattaponga beach although it should be noted that many of them are ex-US Army and can be a little difficult to control, especially for those not used to handling **rocket-assisted machinery**. One hour costs 5500p although much of this is often spent entangled in high voltage electricity wires.

> ### Traveller's Tip
> Visitors should take care on the beaches of Thong On as many of the region's lifeguards are privately employed by local resorts and will only rescue guests who wave a clearly identifiable room key.

Snorkeling has fallen victim to local land-clearing and options are a little limited, as much of the coast along Pattaponga is turbid deltaic swamp. However, keen divers can take a day trip out to feel their way round the sludge beds of Tek Kon. Tour operators provide all the gear: mask, fins, torch and shovel.

This traditional way of carrying produce is not only practical but 'Sun-smart'.

The Yu Nong Straits

The Straits of Yu Nong off Phaic Tan's west coast are enormously popular with divers who come each year to explore the many wrecks that lie beneath its tropical waters. Over 50 separate ships have sunk within this narrow stretch of sea, many running aground on unmarked atolls or failing to negotiate the Straits' treacherous **reef system**. Others were simply victims of the Phaic Tanese navy's entrenched tendency to shoot first, issue an official denial later.

The stunning coves and headlands of this magnificent coastline were first discovered in 1534 by Dutch explorer Ruud van Hootman, who wrote...

'I am so taken with its charms that I have alighted and made gift with musket. This evokes great delight and smiles. They may be the friendliest peoples I've thus met and so agreeable that...'

This was his last entry. A brilliant navigator, van Hootman was however a very poor judge of character and was shot with the musket. His charts are still used today.

T H O N G   O

PHAIC

GREAT

Point Hope   Pt Take

El Quedo A South American-registered freighter, the *El Quedo* suffered mechanical problems while crossing the Straits in 1967. The Captain fired an emergency flare that came back down on the ship's deck, causing it to burn and sink within minutes.

HMS Stonehaven A cargo vessel of 498 tons, the *Stonehaven* sank in 1935 leaving only two survivors. They were John Pearce, a deckhand who clung to an up-turned lifeboat, and Freda Dodds who clung to a chicken coop. A third passenger, Aiden Jeffries, clung to an anchor and was never seen again.

The Yu Nong Straits are a designated Marine Protection Zone. No commercial fishing or removal of coral except after dark.

El Quedo

SS Ontago

Wet Sok Is

Shipping Alert Even though a lighthouse was built on Wet Sok Island in 1965, due to budgetary constraints, it only flashes once a month.

MS Stonehaven

SS Ontago A US-registered passenger liner, in 1943 the *Ontago* was converted to a destroyer. Attempting to cross the Yu Nong Straits a few months later it was hit by several torpedoes, at which point the *Ontago* was converted to a submarine.

Khravat Is

Y U   N O N G   S

Ban Mi

Na Chok Is

Khapak Island This bleak, windswept island was once a leper colony. The colony was closed in 1954 and Khapak Island is now used as a children's holiday camp.

Khapak Is

Koh Samosa One of the most beautiful islands in the Yu Nong Straits. Koh Samosa was actually visited by naturalist Charles Darwin who, despite failing to discover any new animal species, did become the first member of the British Royal Society to have his beard braided.

Koh Samosa Is

Mt Siyuden

PIRATES Boat owners should be aware that piracy is still a major problem in the Yu Nong Straits, despite government attempts to stamp it out. In fact, over recent years some local operators have actually embraced the practice as a tourist attraction, offering visitors the chance to join a pirate ship for a unique special-interest cruise. Costs are high – around US$5000 a week – but much of this amount can be made up for in stolen goods.

Pattaponga

RD

Point Tribulation

The **SS Atlas** left Pattaponga and entered the Straits in 1956 carrying almost 500 tons of coal, an ambitious cargo load for a fibreglass catamaran. It sank within minutes.

Kru Kut Bay

USS Maryanne During military manoeuvres in 1943 a Spitfire running low on fuel attempted to land on the deck of this ship. Unfortunately, the *Maryanne* was not an aircraft carrier, but a small patrol boat, and sank within minutes.

GREAT

SS Atlas

USS Maryanne

El Lobos A magnificent galleon, this ship was under the control of Spain's most incompetent navigator Juan de Carlos who came through here in 1568 searching for his reading glasses.

Warning Due to powerful currents, strong winds and highly variant tides, visitors are warned about attempting a crossing of the Straits in a dinghy or canoe hired from U-Sail Boat rentals.

Pt Lefreq

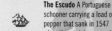
El Lobos

The Escudo A Portuguese schooner carrying a load of pepper that sank in 1547 when the captain sneezed.

The Escudo

The Narrows Numerous vessels can be found here in about 40m of water, the result of an 18th-century tradition in which captains celebrated a successful passage with an on-board fireworks display.

awlung Is

Mawlung Island Dominated by a massive volcano, Mawlung is a popular holiday resort for locals who sail here to enjoy fishing and hunting. The volcano is extinct, as is most of the island's animal population.

Point Despair

NAHKTHONG DELTA

The Curaveca

The Curaveca A Malaysian-registered passenger liner that attempted to cross the Straits in 1977 carrying a group of beauty pageant contestants to the Miss Asia Quest. The vessel hit a shallow reef and its crew abandoned ship, but the captain insisted on going down with his passengers.

ITS

Wild Times

Phra Salahng

Wild Times The flagship of a cruise line catering to 18–35 holiday makers, *Wild Times* sank in 1998 when a group of highly intoxicated passengers broke into the wheelhouse and attempted to 'have a go at steering'.

Na Chok Island

Na Chok Island is by far the most popular holiday destination on Phaic Tan's west coast. Every year thousands of tourists come here to enjoy the warm water, **safe sandy beaches** and pristine hinterland. So idyllic is the setting that Na Chok was briefly considered as a location for the 1950s Hollywood film *South Pacific*, missing out only due to an unseasonal explosion in seasnake numbers. (The producers had even specially commissioned a new musical number 'I'm Gonna Wash That Eel Right Out of My Hair'.)

In recent times Na Chok has developed a reputation as an **expensive hang-out** for the rich and famous and visitors here are likely to encounter all sorts of high-flyers – from wealthy industrialists and international movie stars through to **rogue currency traders**. But despite this emphasis on opulence, Na Chok continues to welcome budget travellers and families – provided they don't intend on staying. The island itself is quite small, about 13 kilometres long and 2 kilometres wide. Na Chok is a very **low lying** stretch of land, the highest point actually a pile of rubble out back of a recently demolished hotel.

The first foreigners to discover Na Chok were probably **Catholic missionaries** who visited during the late 17th century. One of these, a Spanish priest by the name of Father Gancho, wrote that the island was 'largely inhabited by young women, many of rough character and prone to promenading along the beach in various states of undress'. Within a year there were over 700 missionaries on the island, spreading religion through baptism, preaching and general laying on of hands.

SHIP AHOY!

Down at the pier you might be lucky enough to see local Pattapongan boat builders hard at work making their traditional craft. Known as *klunks*, these boats are believed to be the only maritime vessels in the world carved entirely out of stone. The magnificent (if somewhat cumbersome) craft are understandably

lacking in buoyancy and require enormous skill just to keep them afloat. Turning one without capsizing is almost impossible, perhaps explaining why Pattapongan sailors only ever made one-way trips. Sadly, only a few *klunks* still sail, the majority of the fleet having been broken up by prison gangs and turned into paperweights.

The first famous visitor to Na Chok was English naval officer **Captain Albury Potter** who travelled here in 1769 to observe the **Transit of Venus**. Unfortunately he got his dates wrong and missed the astronomical event but he did manage to see a parrot.

Beach hawkers on Na Chok have moved with the times and now, in addition to hair braiding and foot massage, many offer on-the-spot sashimi.

Popular Destination

As Na Chok's reputation as an idyllic getaway grew, so too did visitor numbers. During the early 20th century cruise liners began regularly docking here to disgorge their contents, both passengers and bilge, and in 1917 the **first resort** was built on the island's north coast, followed a year later by a fried chicken outlet.

It was off this stretch of shoreline in 1938 that surfing was supposedly introduced to Phaic Tan by an American visitor **Chad Murdoch** who rode the waves every day until he was mistaken for a dolphin by the crew of a passing fishing trawler and accidentally harpooned.

In 1987 there was an attempt to build an **international airport** on Na Chok's western side but this soon closed down after visiting pilots refused to land on any strip involving a dog-leg turn and mangroves.

Coconuts

Apart from tourism, Na Chok is famous for its **coconuts**, the fruit of which is highly prized. To assist with harvest, monkeys are trained to climb the trees and shake them off. In 1992 the industry was almost brought to its knees when these monkeys went on strike. New **employment contracts** were hastily negotiated and the monkeys returned to the job but they now represent one of the most heavily unionized workforces in Phaic Tan.

PEAK SEASON

Being a tourist island, rates vary from season to season so it's worth checking ahead. As a general rule, peak charges on Na Chok extend from November to October with lower prices only on offer for visitors arriving between midnight and 2.30am on the 5th of November.

Getting There

A ferry leaves Pattaponga wharf each day at 11.00am and generally runs aground on rocks off the island about two hours later. The trip may of course take longer in strong winds or if the captain decides to dangle a line. **Bookings** are essential as the ship is only licensed to carry 200 passengers or livestock and once this number is reached no one else may board unless they're prepared to hide in the **life boats**.

HEALTH ALERT

Visitors can leave their bug spray at home – Na Chok is the only part of Phaic Tan to be mosquito-free. An intensive aerial spraying during the 1970s completely wiped out the insect population and local officials proudly boast that since then not one resident has contracted malaria or managed to fall pregnant.

Flying

There are also flights available to Na Chok on board local operator Noh Air but these are often cancelled due to poor conditions, such as when the pilots turn up for work hung-over. **Bookings** are recommended, as is **life insurance**.

The east coast of Na Chok Island provides magnificent waves and each April surfers arrive in droves for the pre-monsoon swells. Most popular breaks are Jawdropper (a left-hander), Sulaimen (a right-hander) and the Splitz (a left- and right-hander) that should only be attempted by the ambidexterous.

Zou Kow Bow Beach This stunning beach, with what is regarded as the whitest sand in the world, was formed last century by the rare combination of global warming and a huge spill from a tanker carrying laundry bleach.

Where to Stay

For such a small island, there's a wonderful range of places to stay on Na Chok, although it should be noted that the place is not particularly suited to budget travellers. You will find one or two **youth hostels** on the rocky east coast but their remote location and active drug police tend to deter all but the most determined of backpackers. The fact is, Na Chok is about wealth, and here you will find some of the most exclusive **luxury resorts** in the world. Set amid lush rainforest, these places all boast heavily uniformed guards who are employed to keep hawkers and other undesirables from disturbing the guests. Though their tactics may at times appear somewhat heavy-handed (see our section on the **Ramada Inn Massacre**), the fact is these folk are not worth messing with.

$$$ Expensive

✉ 32 Chok Chok Lu
☎ 39 573 996
@ sands@phalti.com.pt
▤ DC MC V
 pool
 gym
 live music

Shangri La Sands Considered by many to be the finest resort on Na Chok, if not the entire country, the Shangri La Sands offers the ultimate in beachfront luxury. The resort boasts a staff of over 1500 and, with a maximum of just eight guests at any time, the attention is constant if a little overwhelming. Guests arriving at reception will be greeted by a full symphony orchestra playing an arrival overture especially composed for the occasion. Accommodation is provided in authentic bures or small thatched cottages modeled on traditional village huts, except for the fact they're three-storey glass and chrome palaces.

Jonathan Writes... *For the Luxury Traveller*

I've always enjoyed my sojourns at the Shangri-La. The staff are *très excellent* and manage to strike that perfect balance between due diligence and abject grovelling. Sadly on my last visit I struggled to muster a complaint. Fortunately, on my final day, I returned from a stunning *petit déjeuner* of lobster bisque to find the lavatory paper had not been folded into a symmetrical triangular tip. I insisted that a mathematician be brought in to teach the staff the proper proportions.

Na Chok Health Oasis Resort For the ultimate in spa retreats, the Oasis combines healthy living with five-star luxury. Soothing ambient music plays in the lobby while a large fountain shoots jets of Evian water into the air. Guests can take advantage of numerous health and beauty treatments including yoga, meditation, chi kung, herbal steam facials, body wraps and dermabrasion in which the outer layers of skin are gently removed with a blow-torch. For those into alternative therapies there's an Holistic Healing Centre where you can attend talks on past lives* or be helped to find your inner child – although you will be charged for an extra seat should he/she make an appearance. Naturally enough the Resort's four restaurants are all vegetarian (even the steakhouse) and no alcohol is permitted, which reduces your chances of being bothered by Australian tourists.

✉ *57 Suahu Lu*
☎ *39 924 459*
@ *nachok@phalti.com.pt*
▤ *DC MC V*
  pool
  gym
  dermabrasion available

* **Be Warned** *Local police can still arrest you for what you did in a past life.*

Part of the prestigious Royal Lilo chain, **The Wilted Orchid** is another six-star resort situated on the west coast of the island. Suites here are all sumptuous, featuring special touches such as a marble horizon bath covered in cut crocus flowers and handwoven silk shower caps. Of course, being in such a remote location not everything works perfectly and in some of the honeymoon suites the remote-control drapes are noise activated and have a tendency to open without warning. A range of massage treatments are available to guests staying at the Orchid, including shiatsu, deep tissue and 'extremely deep tissue', a type of tactile therapy that can only be performed under anaesthetic.

✉ *34 Thanon Tralanhng*
☎ *39 673 223*
@ *wilted@phoni.com.pt*
▤ *DC V*
  gym
  restaurant

One of Na Chok's newest resort complexes, **Kayhanma** sits on an isolated isthmus at the island's northern tip. It's so secluded that there is no road in – all guests arrive by helicopter. Once checked in to this luxurious oasis there is no need to walk, as the entire resort is criss-crossed by travelators. Guests may control the temperature, not only in their own room but outside, thanks to a special sky dome that creates its own micro-climate. Considered by many the ultimate honeymoon destination, every need is taken care of at Kayhanma. And if you're single they'll even provide a complimentary spouse.

✉ *38 Thanon Tralanhng*
☎ *39 452 223*
@ *kayhanma@phoni.com.pt*
▤ *DC V*
  restaurant

⊠ *74 Chok Chok Lu*
☏ *39 000 238*
@ *lodge@phoni.com.pt*
▤ *MC V*
   pool
   gym
   restaurant

Sun Lodge   Many people come to Sun Lodge for the pool alone, a massive body of water landscaped exquisitely into the surrounding gardens. Reclining on an inflatable mattress in the centre of this pool, the view frames lush, rolling lawns cascading down to the sparkling sea. A small village and hospital had to be demolished to achieve this stunning vista, but that's the hallmark of resorts like this. In terms of activities, Sun Lodge offers everything for the stressed out tourist and there's a state of the art gymnasium where you can work up a sweat or – for a small extra fee – pay one of the staff members to do so on your behalf. Activities include the usual water sports and guests get free use of the resort's 40-foot yacht, a magnificent vessel that comes complete with its own 3-foot skipper.

$ Not So Expensive

⊠ *163 Suahu Lu*
☏ *39 865 690*
▤ *DC MC V*

Ocean Green   Despite being set a little back from the beach, this relaxed complex occupies a fabulous position and boasts an impressive pool-slide – although, oddly, no pool. The cottages all feature thatched roofs or, at least, they did until last year's hurricane season. Many of the rooms have wonderful views, if you're prepared to stand on a chair and use your imagination.

⊠ *26 Thanon Tralanhng*
☏ *39 663 209*
@ *dak@phoni.com.pt*
▤ *DC*

Dak Bay Villas   Another good value option, this is one of the island's larger resorts; 56 units face the ocean while another 40 out back face demolition. There are air-conditioners in all the rooms but, due to limited power supplies on Na Chok island, turning them on involves cutting power at the local hospital. Prices naturally reflect beachside proximity, but even the more distant rooms have rotting seaweed dumped outside each night for that authentic olfactory experience.

Padmai Hotel Marketing itself as a 'family friendly' holiday resort, the Padmai has no shortage of beach and poolside activities. But its main attraction is the hugely popular Kids Club where vacationing parents can drop their children for the morning, day or – with advance notice – a couple of months. It's a little costly but reduced fees can be negotiated if your off-spring are willing to perform basic manual labour.

✉ *27 Chok Chok Lu*
☎ *39 220 502*
▤ *MC V*
pool

The Na Chok Reef Budget Resort Situated at the southern tip of the island, this place offers good sized bungalows directly opposite where the beach used to be before it was washed away. Rooms are a little on the small side and there are no window screens but this doesn't matter as there are no windows. Many visitors come to the Reef for the express purpose of learning to scuba dive. They specialize in teaching absolute beginners and the instructors are very understanding with guests who can't swim as neither can many of them.

✉ *94 Suahu Lu*
☎ *39 522 596*
▤ *DC V*

The Na Chok Reef Resort boasts one of the most popular (legal) nude beaches in Phaic Tan, a secluded cover where guests may swim and relax 'au natural'. This beach is also one of the few places in the world where it is possible to have one's pubic hair braided by discrete resort staff.

Where to Eat

If you're staying at one of the more exclusive or secluded resorts on the island, chances are you'll eat there. In fact, many of these places make this a stipulation and guests caught dining 'AWOL' may legally be forced back their resort restaurants at gunpoint and made to order dessert.

But if you do choose to sample one of Na Chok's many restaurants, you'll enjoy a wonderful range of food and drink. Not surprisingly, seafood features heavily, even in meat dishes, thanks to the local islander's love of *nergak* (fermented shrimp paste), a pungent concoction added to just about every dish. The precise recipe for *nergak* remains shrouded in secrecy but would seem to involve taking jars of normal shrimp paste and leaving them in the sun for several days.

✉ *74 Chok Chok Lu*
☎ *39 532 255*
▤ *DC V*
   live music

Breezes With stunning harbour views and an extensive menu, Breezes would have to be *the* place to enjoy fine seafood on Na Chok. Exotic dishes include crab, braised shark's fin, bruised shark's fin and the restaurant's signature dish, Kingdom of the Deep, featuring a half lobster served with prawns and squid on a rusty anchor.

✉ *86 Suahu Lu*

Lai Yuen The latest in trendy beachside dining, this funky new cafe attracts diners from all over the island. The food is great but the place is outrageously understaffed, with about one waitress to 40 tables. The poor girl does a great job but this doesn't stop her being subjected to a stream of abuse from the owner who sits behind the counter barking orders. It's a good thing they're married.

✉ *37 Thanon Tralanhng*
☎ *39 686 990*
▤ *DC*

Of course, it's not all seafood on Na Chok and 'carnivores' will enjoy a night out at **Chuak**, an up-market, yet relaxed restaurant specializing in meat. Its extensive menu is written in Phaic Tanese but each dish is illustrated by photos depicting, not just the finished meal, but the precise manner in which it was slaughtered.

Note *Those dining with young children should avoid showing them the lamb or rabbit sections.*

Jonathan Writes... *For the Luxury Traveller* After numerous recommendations I finally managed to book a table at Lai Yuen and sat down on my specially reinforced seat to enjoy their much vaunted cuisine. Imagine my disappointment when the maitre'd announced that the tiger prawns lightly infused in truffle oil were not available due to a local fishing boat capsizing with the loss of all on board. If a dining establishment is not capable of delivering listed menu items then it simply does not deserve to be operating. After a disappointingly over-salted plate of scallops I had a jolly good mind not to pay the bill until I remembered that, as a fine food reviewer, I never do. Very poor form.

Bistro Sombreroh A good mid-priced dining option, Bistro Sombreroh is open seven days a week (except Monday, Wednesday, maybe Thursday and most of the weekend). Specializing in South American cuisine, the meals are panfried tableside, which makes for a great spectacle as the chef flamboyantly tosses food around and then attempts to extinguish the linen. Service can be a little slow (diners have reported ordering veal only to have it arrive as aged beef), but prices are good and a large – if somewhat noisy – air-conditioning unit just about manages to drown out the sound of Sombreroh's resident salsa band.

✉ *90 Suahu Lu*
☎ *39 682 100*
live music

As a rule most people on Na Chok go to bed early but if you are looking for a bit of nightclubbing action, head to **Palmz!** on the main Esplanade. This funky disco-cum-bar is downstairs in a large basement and gets pretty crowded on weekends. One word of caution – if you're on the dance floor and the smoke machine starts filling the place with fumes, evacuate immediately. Palmz! nightclub does not have a smoke machine.

✉ *133 Chok Chok Lu*
live music

DEEP SEA DELICACY

One of the most sought after creatures on Na Chok is a local marine species called chiuk dihn, *an abalone-like shellfish that thrives in the murky, nutrient-rich waters off-shore.* Chiuk dihn *must be tenderized by hitting it repeatedly with a metal mallet. After several hours of this process the fish is then killed and boiled in vinegar before being sliced and sold to make light-weight body armour.*

Attractions

If you come to Na Chok then chances are you're here to enjoy the island's many beautiful and **secluded beaches**. Here you can lie back on a deckchair in the shade of an illegally tall hotel while sipping a curdled yogurt cocktail or cut loose with a range of water-based activities such as jet skiing, windsurfing or just being rescued from any one of the coastline's many **treacherous rips**.

The diving off Na Chok is excellent and operators such as **Neptune Underwater Safaris** will take small groups (6–8 people) out to the reef and then bring most of them (4–6 people) back. Numerous other dive outfits provide services on the island and one of them, **LearnFast**, even offers full PADI certificates in just five minutes (cash only). The most popular dive site to visit is *The Bahtra*, a rusting military submarine that sits a few kilometres off Na Chok's west coast, except for those times when it's called away on naval maneouvres.

Visitors staying on the south or western side of the island should be aware that the beaches here can get a little dangerous due to **strong currents** and numerous hidden rips. Pay close attention to swimming warnings and signs, such as the local lifeguard floating face down off-shore, and avoid going any deeper than your knees unless attached to the beach with some form of **harness**.

Note *Nude bathing is permitted at many of Na Chok's more up-market resorts although gentlemen swimming after 6pm may be required to wear a tie.*

Resort staff at one of Na Chok's private beaches search for a guest's missing contact lens.

Of course, if all this activity gets too much you can always order another cocktail and settle back on your deck chair with a good book. The only problem here is the large number of persistent beach hawkers who patrol the beach, bombarding holiday makers with offers of **hair braiding**, scalp massage, toe-nail painting or, more recently, colonic irrigation. Once targeted it's almost impossible to get rid of these touts who will interrupt just about any activity to push their wares. **Scuba diving** used to be one means of escape but recently several determined operators armed with aqualungs have begun setting up **souvenir stalls** on the sea-bed.

By far the country's most loved animal (and national symbol), the Phaic Tanese Terrier – known locally as Yapyap – is the world's smallest working dog. Bred to round up squirrels, the Yapyap is so highly-strung that it is not uncommon for vets to prescribe beachside vacations and Prozac shakes.

If you wander along any of Na Chok's beaches shortly after dawn you'll see an unusual and magical sight – local fishermen perched on posts thrashing the water with long bamboo poles attached to a small net. Known as *thrahk-on*, this **age-old technique** has been practiced by these simple folk for generations and, despite no evidence that anyone has ever caught a fish, the tradition lives on.

Many visitors to this part of Phaic Tan have complained about the dozens of **jet skis** that buzz by the shore, shattering the peace and creating hazards for other boat owners. Local authorities have attempted to solve the problem by limiting certain stretches to boats with masts but some **unscrupulous operators** have begun designing jet skis to look like sailing boats. They are, however, easy to pick as yachts rarely break the 100km/h barrier.

OCEAN SAFETY

Despite years of over-fishing, the waters round Na Chok Island are still full of nasty creatures such as stonefish and stingrays. Stepping on these creatures can be very painful and even lead to respitory paralysis. If you are stung, remain calm and, if possible, try to keep the wound well below the level of your heart. If you happen to be stung on the head this may involve a series of handstands. For jellyfish stings the best treatment is to douse the wound in vinegar. Bottles are placed along most public beaches while up-market resorts will offer a choice of balsamic or cider.

Ban Mi Island

Lacking the lush, tropical splendour of nearby Na Chok Island, Ban Mi is actually situated in a **rain shadow** and, as a consequence, tends to be extremely arid. One positive of this is that your water-based activities are unlikely to be interrupted by rain although they may be somewhat limited due to **dehydration**.

Historically, Europeans never found much of economic value on Ban Mi so they barely bothered with the island. A brief moment of international excitement occurred in the mid-1970s when a British exploration company working off the island's eastern tip thought they'd struck **oil**, only to discover that they'd drilled into a sunken container of **tanning lotion**.

A favourite of backpackers and intrepid travelers, Ban Mi again made the headlines some years ago when rebels fighting for independence raided a resort and attempted to take several dozen guests hostage, only to be forced back by staff members armed with blow-darts made from **cocktail umbrellas**.

Boasting only a handful of burgeoning tourist resorts and limited activities, Ban Mi is ideal for the traveler who wants to sit back and do nothing because, put simply, there's nothing to do. The pace here is slow and about the only time you'll see someone hurry is when you ask a waiter for the bill.

Nightlife on Ban Mi is pretty much non-existent and there's little in the way of organized tours, however the beaches are magnificently clean, if a little sandless, and the island's scrubby limestone plateaus do have their own unique, **wind-swept charm**.

Ban Mi Island *What it lacks in beaches it more than makes up for in exposed rock.*

When to Go

If you're coming for the beach or water sports it's important to get your timing right. Mid-September through to the end of December is the **windiest time** on Ban Mi. The seas are choppy and **underwater visibility** so poor that even the fish struggle to find their way around.

Getting There

There are about half a dozen companies that provide a **ferry service** from Pattaponga to Ban Mi and, while this competition does keep prices down, it has led to some unnecessary and often dangerous attempts by various boat captains to out-do each other. As a rule, avoid any service described as 'express' or 'rocket'.

Remember, there is no ferry terminal on the island and at low tide passengers may be required to disembark several hundred metres off shore and wade through **tidal sludge**.

For those with less time to spare, the island can also be reached by speedboat. These **light-weight aluminium craft** dart across the narrow passage in about half an hour and the trip will cost you around 5000p, although this figure is somewhat deceptive as you must add in the price of chiropractic after-care and anti-inflamatories.

At many of Ban Mi's resorts staff seniority is indicated by the size of one's sunglasses.

Sven Writes...
For the Budget Traveller

Getting to Ban Mi can be dead cheap if you're prepared to hitch a ride on one of the many fishing trawlers that operate off-shore. Most pass within 500m of the island's northern tip and if you're a reasonably good swimmer you can reach the beach in half an hour, saving yourself a ferry ticket fee of 35p (US 12 cents).

Communications

After years of being somewhat cut off from the outside world Ban Mi has finally entered the 21st century with the opening of its first **internet café**. For just a few hundred pong visitors can now sit down at one of its two computer terminals and try logging on. They won't succeed as the café is not yet connected to the outside world but it is possible to send emails from one of the computers to the other. Any other **emails** will be printed out and taken on the next inter-island ferry (allow six working days).

Where to Stay

Most hotels and resorts on Ban Mi are clustered along the south coast of the island where the **limestone cliffs** provide some protection from prevailing winds. There is also some accommodation available on the western side but it's pretty limited and visitors planning a stay there should bring basic supplies such as their own roof and walls.

In addition to luxury resorts and hotels, several tour companies offer '**home stay**' packages where you live with a local island family and share in their daily life. These should be booked with caution as there's a fine line between 'guest' and 'hostage'.

As a general guide, you can get a room with fan on Ban Mi for about 1000p per night. A room without a fan will set you back 500–750p. A fan without a room is yours for 200p but you will need somewhere to hang it.

Feigning sleep or even unconsciousness will not deter the average Ban Mi beach tout, some of whom have been known to wait several months for a sale.

$$$ Expensive

The Royal Grand One of Ban Mi's first and finest luxury resorts, the Royal is an imposing building looking out across Chek Weh Bay. From its sumptuous day beds guests can gaze out over water turning from azure green to cobalt blue to Exon brown while sipping one of the most watered-down cocktails in the world. The Royal offers a wide range of guest activities such as snooker, sailing, swimming, yoga and small bore pistol shooting. Note, however, the resort has recently discontinued its fruit carving classes after a guest held up reception using an extremely realistic-looking pistol made out of lychees.

12 Thanon
Chek Weh
39 582 004
DC MC V
pool
gym
small bore pistol
shooting available

Tropical Links Villas Fore! Featuring its very own Nick Faldo designed golf course (or at least, a bootleg version thereof), the Links is one of Ban Mi's most popular resorts. Suites are all large and from the bathrooms you have a wonderful view of golfers making their way along the third hole. Somewhat disconcertingly, they have a similar view of you as curtains and shutters are not yet installed. Tropical Links boasts a full cable TV service, including CNN, CNN Asia and a special CNN channel dedicated solely to the resort itself. At the flick of a switch guests can be updated on their own personal stocks, weather conditions and how far off your room service order is from being delivered.

75 Tan Mi Donglu
39 233 042
DC MC V
golf course

Phuan Li Another top-end resort on the island's south coast, guests arriving at Phuan Li will be greeted by female staff members who will place a floral wreath round your neck. This serves as not only a ceremonial welcome but also a personal tracking device, deemed necessary after several people went missing in the hotel's extensively landscaped gardens. The rooms all have excellent views and feature CD and video disk players, two-line speaker phones with voice mail, surround stereo system, air-conditioning, automatic curtains – everything you could possibly want, with the possible exception of electricity, which tends to be somewhat erratic. Phuan Li boasts several pools and its own private beach that, like the concierge's smile, is artificial.

174 Phat So
Suahu Lu
39 683 567
DC MC
restaurant

$ Not So Expensive

✉ *15 Tan Mi Donglu*

The Ban Mi Holiday Villas A 4-hectare complex south of the ferry terminal, this bungalow-style resort is well located, especially for lovers of mangrove ecosystems. Rooms here are pretty basic and there are no showers; however, much of the overhead plumbing leaks so it's easy to keep clean. Some of the cheaper rooms have no windows so specify if you're fond of natural light or a minimum oxygen concentration.

✉ *12 Thanon Chek Weh*
☎ *39 678 243*
▤ *DC MC V*

Kum Ling Resort An excellent place to stay for those who enjoy water sports, Kum Ling is right on the coast and boasts its own private beach. While at low tide the water can be quite a few hundred metres off shore, around high tide guests wanting to swim won't have to go much further than the hotel lobby. For those interested in things cultural, not far from the resort are traditional huts where residents live in makeshift cottages without water or electricity. These are the staff quarters.

✉ *63 Tan Mi Donglu*
☎ *39 684 229*
▤ *DC V*
   pool

Phul Yruk Guest House is a plain two-storey wooden house with rooms starting at 400p per night. Simple and clean, it has everything you need, including mosquito nets and a jar of aloe vera for scorpion bites. Every room has a view, usually of the back laneway, and a range of activities such as windsurfing, parasailing and jet skiing are offered although, being some 5km inland, these take place in the hotel pool.

Traveller's Tip

Day-trippers should remember that most of Ban Mi's resorts feature private beaches and non-guests caught swimming or sunbathing here may legally be pushed back into the ocean. 👍

A SHADY PAST!

One of Ban Mi's most famous (or perhaps infamous) resorts would have to be the **Ocean View Villas**. Built about 10 years ago by a consortium made up of Pattaponga-based criminals and medical specialists, the project ran into trouble when guests complained that none of the rooms actually had a view of the ocean, due to a thick stand of remnant rainforest between the resort and the coast. An application to chop this rainforest down was rejected by planning authorities at which point the vegetation began to mysteriously disappear. The resort owners blamed 'global warming' but the nightly sound of double-handed saws and bulldozers prompted authorities to finally step in. Several officials from the Environmental Protection Board were sent to investigate and their interim report is believed to contain some damning accusations. However, this report was destroyed, along with its authors, when the boat carrying them back to the mainland accidentally hit an un-marked torpedo (later blamed, somewhat unconvincingly, on Al Qaeda). A memorial to the men was erected in front of the Ocean View Villas but removed several weeks later after guests complained it was blocking their view. That said the vista is stunning.

Where to Eat

Due to its distance from the mainland and irregular supply ships, don't expect the food on Ban Mi to be the freshest. Salads will usually feature, not just dried tomatoes, but **dried lettuce**, and bread can often only be sliced with the aid of a **cross-cut saw**. But this doesn't mean you won't eat well on Ban Mi and there are numerous restaurants to sample. Walk along the main esplanade any afternoon and you'll be struck by the smell of **roasting meat** coming from a local café or sunbaking British backpacker.

While beer is freely available on Ban Mi, imported wines tend to be limited and a little on the expensive side. As for champagne, it is now officially banned due to the generally rough ocean crossings that recently saw a cargo ship loaded with Dom Perignon explode at sea. Rescue attempts claimed another six lives, all of whom died from alcohol poisoning.

BOTTOMS UP!
You can't possibly visit the island without lashing out on its signature cocktail, a Ban Mi Sling. At US$25 a pop it's not cheap, but you're bound to enjoy this exotic blend of rum, vodka, gin, vermouth, schnapps, bourbon, ouzo, formaldehyde and lime juice. There is a kid's version available in which they omit the gin.

The Ban Mi seafood market specializes in hukmon or 'flattened fish', a local delicacy made by backing over salmon with a tractor.

Mirsing Seafood Restaurant This place is bright and features extensive lunch and dinner menus, as well as monthly themes. Come in April when it's 'Empty the Ashtrays' month or just take pot luck. The place is generally packed and owner Mr Mirsing holds court from behind his bar with endless charm although some diners wanting to split the bill have reported a dark side.

✉ *42 Tan Mi Donglu*
☎ *39 862 600*
▤ *DC MC V*

Sea Breezes Overlooking the water, this stylish bistro has an unmistakable tropical feel, from the rattan furniture to the cockroaches in its kitchen. On weekends Sea Breezes features a local island band playing traditional folk tunes so if you enjoy good music book a table outside and bring a walkman.

✉ *78 Thanon Chek Weh*
☎ *39 673 552*
▤ *DC V*
outdoor dining
live music

Ban Mi Beach Bistro This noisy, beachfront restaurant is not far from the main ferry terminal and serves a wide range of buffet-style meals. If you're after succulent seafood in elegant surroundings it's worth making a reservation – somewhere else. But if it's quick food at a reasonable price you're after, this is it.

✉ *16 Phat So Suahu Lu*
☎ *39 678 499*
▤ *MC V*

Bamboo House The only Chinese restaurant on the island, Bamboo House specializes in 'steamboat', a fondue-style meal in which diners place chunks of fish and meat into boiling broth at their table. A helpful waiter stands by to offer assistance and first aid for those who suffer serious scalding.

✉ *73 Tan Mi Donglu*
☎ *39 868 229*
▤ *DC V*

Casa Luna Another 'ethnic' eatery on the island, this bistro claims to offer an authentic taste of Italy. The menu features offerings such as *prosciutto e melone* (a melon ball wrapped in processed meat) and large plates of *spaghetti al fungi* (spaghetti with fungus). Casa Luna also boasts one of the largest pepper grinders in the world – it takes three waiters to lift it. Homesick Italians will enjoy authentic touches such as the fat, sweaty chef threatening his staff with genuine stand-over tactics and the checked red and white table clothes, even if these are actually plain white linen splattered with sauce and, in some cases, blood stains.

✉ *25 Thanon Chek Weh*
▤ *DC*

Visitors Note The entire coastal region off Ban Mi is a designated marine park, meaning you're not allowed to fish, spear fish, net, trawl or remove coral within view of anyone else.

Attractions

As with many of the islands in this region, a lot of visitors want to do nothing more than settle back and relax on the beach. Sun lovers should however keep in mind that on Ban Mi nudity is only permitted in certain areas, mainly below the knees. Remember, also, that many beaches on the island are privately owned and that deckchairs lined up on these stretches are likely to be electrified.

Snorkeling is very popular on the island, with a huge range of marine life to be found in the shallows, including sea snakes, stingrays, cone fish, stone fish, box jellies, moray eels, bristle worms and stinging anemones. In fact, Ban Mi boasts more venomous creatures per cubic metre than any other ocean in the world. Even those who remain on the shore are not completely safe due to local species such as *pergani*, a blue-ringed octopus that can actually travel several kilometres inland in search of human flesh.

Of course, for more interesting underwater sites, you'll need to take a trip off shore to places such as the **Kuan Prem Reef**. This site is enormously popular with divers, over 50 of whom drown here each year. Underwater you can view massive schools of spectacular tropical fish. Please do not feed them – although tips are appreciated by some of the larger coral species.

Another popular dive site is **Kakop Island**, (right) a rocky outcrop surrounded by a series of coral knolls some 5km off Ban Mi's eastern shores. It has a unique coral

system and international marine scientists were aghast when they learned in 1981 that it would be used for target practice by the Phaic Tanese Air Force. The Air Force were similarly aghast when, in over 200 bombing sorties, they failed to hit the island once. The Air Force responded by finding much larger targets in the nearby rainforests and using cluster bombs, thus preserving the pristine beauty of Kakop Island for all time.

If you don't know how to scuba dive then Ban Mi is a great place to learn however several disreputable **diving schools** have sprung up in recent times. Be wary of any dive boat that appears to be fitted out with used LPG cylinders and/or lengths of garden hose. No matter what operator you choose to learn with, remember the scuba fundamentals: stay within a safe depth, always dive with a buddy and never leave your wallet back on the boat.

BEAT THE DRUM

In the days before roads were built across the island, drums were used as a traditional form of communication between villages and a way of bringing people together. It worked like this – one village would sound its drum, members of a neighbouring village would then come over and tell them to shut up and before long a violent dispute would break out. These drums, called *buangum*, are made from hollowed out logs, 60cm in diameter, and covered in taut beagle hide. In July there is a drum festival when teams of *buangum* players compete. The loudest drummer is declared the winner and then banished.

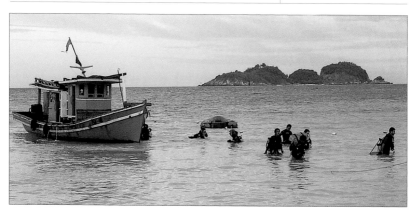

Scuba diving students off Ban Mi search for their instructor.

For those wanting to truly get away from it all, consider a trek across the island to **Mek Sung Cove**. Situated on the west coast, this beach is truly isolated and those visiting should be prepared to live like Robinson Crusoe – i.e. with another man – as it's a popular gay haunt.

In the center of the island you'll find a series of limestone caves at the foot of a craggy escarpment. The largest of these, **Lai Ching Cave**, contains several carvings of Buddha and other interesting sights. Entrance is free but an optional 500p donation is worth considering, especially if you wish to see the outside world again.

Like Senchok Beach back on the mainland, **Tengah Beach** on the island's northern side used to be famous as one of the few sites in the world where giant leatherback turtles would come ashore once a year to lay their eggs. Sadly, these magnificent giants of the deep have stopped using the beach, driven away by persistent touts attempting to sell them T-shirts.

If the kids have had enough of beach life for a while, consider a visit to **Aquabeat**, the island's newly opened swimming complex. Apart from the usual slides and diving ramps, Aquabeat has its own wave pool where the youngsters can pretend they're 'hanging five' on a surfboard or clinging to a capsized ferry.

The Aquabeat outdoor swimming complex. Come on the first weekend of each month when the water is re-chlorinated.

Many westerners come to Ban Mi seeking spiritual enlightenment and leave with deep-vein thrombosis.

04

Phaic Tăn
Pha Phlung

Introduction

No trip to Phaic Tan would be complete without visiting the exotic northern province of Pha Phlung. A region of stunning **natural beauty**, the rainforests of Pha Phlung are known for their cool climate, secluded waterfalls and **spectacular mudslides**.

This area is traditionally known as the 'Land of a Thousand Tigers' and, while actual numbers may be closer to seven (counting five in the Lom Buak Grand Circus), **guided nature walks** are still a marvelous opportunity to see nature up close. Here, if you're lucky, you may even catch a glimpse of the region's **floral emblem** the odourless orchid.

Then there's the amazing Chua Wa hydro-electricity plant – regarded by many as one of the **seven unnatural wonders** of the world. How workers managed to haul materials over such inhospitable terrain to construct the **massive dam wall** remained a mystery until recently when engineers revealed they had used pumice stone. The wall itself is now ranked as the most porous man-made structure in the world, as most villagers down-river will attest.

Sven Writes...
For the Budget Traveller

If you're coming north to go trekking there's no need to blow big bucks on a guide. Simply learn to follow footprints then head off a few hours behind a large tour group. With basic tracking skills and a willingness to live rough for a few days you can stumble through some pretty special country on the cheap.

FASCINATING FACT

Remarkably, every city, town and village in eastern Pha Phlung Province was extensively bombed between 1967 and 1978. Even more remarkably, there was no war in the region.

Hill Tribes

But of course, for many it is the people of Pha Phlung that are the region's main attraction and each month thousands of visitors come to get a glimpse at the many unique **Hill Tribes** living here. Many of these simple folk still practise traditional slash-and-burn agriculture, even those living in city townhouses, and a visit is well worth the **painful vaccinations**.

Hill Stations

The province of Pha Phlung covers 21,000 sq km, over 30% of which is covered by rainforest and mountains, the remaining 70% being covered by a **dense haze**, the result of intensive tobacco-growing operations in the eastern district of Bung Lung. Apart from its capital Nham Pong, there's no shortage of fascinating centres to visit in Pha Phlung, from elegant **hill station towns** such as Lokar Huag (elevation 1280m) through to cities buried beneath massive mudslides, such as Doi Mae (elevation minus 156m).

Philippe Writes...
Fifteen years ago Pha Phlung was a war-torn, lawless region where people were dying everyday, victims of malnutrition, disease or bloodshed brought on by rival drug lords fighting for control. Tragically, since then numerous international aid agencies have stepped in to restore peace and raise living standards, thus destroying the very charm that drew seasoned travellers like myself to this region in the first place.

(Left) Locals say the famous Emerald Pools of Pha Phlung get their colour from limestone deposits although scientists suspect it may have something to do with the silk dyeing plant upstream.

TOP CROP
Despite Pha Phlung agricultural authorities banning their rice farmers from using genetically modified seed, considerable suspicion has been aroused because of their ability to produce 12 crops a year, along with the fact that much of the rice produced is blue.

Tina Writes...
On many bus trips through Pha Phlung the driver will often insist on loading your luggage onto the roof. I've heard so many stories of travellers arriving at a destination only to find – surprise, surprise, all bags have mysteriously gone missing. Which is why I insist upon riding on the roof. If this is not possible, I at least consider attaching myself to my suitcase via a specially lengthened set of handcuffs.

The Economy

Pha Phlung was once a great **trade route** between China and the rest of Asia, although the only things exchanged these days are gunfire and rare strains of bird flu. But despite decades of military conflict, the province of Pha Phlung is quite well off, a legacy of its long involvement in the cultivation and sale of **opium poppies**. Obviously, much of this trade is illegal and the local government is working hard to develop more socially acceptable industry alternatives. In the capital Nham Pong a factory has recently been opened where former opium producers are being taught to manufacture Sarin gas. But opium remains an important part of the region's historic and cultural fabric, especially in more remote villages. Here, during the **Harvest Festival**, visitors can still enjoy watching the first of the new season's opium poppies being picked and ceremoniously crushed by young women, often daughters of **local drug lords**.

Land Mines

Pha Phlung Province is one of the most heavily land mined areas on earth and UXO (**unexploded ordnance**) still cover much of the region. Fortunately many are made in Phaic Tan and therefore unlikely to work. The most common UXO found in Pha Phlung are small cluster bombs, blue or grey metal balls about the size of a fist. If you see such an object on the ground, avoid it at all costs. If you find one in your food, think twice about ordering dessert.

The good news for Pha Phlung is that in recent years numerous de-mining organizations have been working hard to clear the land. A French NGO has had limited success with **trained Labradors**; these dogs are very adept at finding mines but have the unfortunate tendency to dig them up and drop them in front of their handler.

When travelling through the countryside it's essential to stay on the trails and only venture further afield if accompanied by a qualified and experienced guide. A guide missing one or more limbs may well be experienced but not 'qualified'.

OPIUM

While technically illegal, many locals still smoke opium and it's hard to travel anywhere in Pha Phlung without coming across reminders of this addiction. Don't be fooled by the contrived image of exotic dens full of artists and poets – there is nothing glamorous about this form of drug addiction. The sight of a sallow-skinned man sucking on a pipe while staring off into space is not a pretty one, especially if he happens to be driving your bus at the time. Long-term opium addicts suffer numerous health problems and most end up living on the streets or eking out a meagre existence as program directors at local FM radio stations.

DRUG DAZE
The local government has fought a long battle with drug lords and bandits. In 1998 they sent several hundred specially trained undercover officers into the hills where it was hoped they could live with the people and gain valuable information on the drug trade. These officers now run one of the largest opium cartels in the province. However, there has been progress in the fight against narcotic producers and, thanks to an increased army presence, many of the region's more powerful and violent drug lords have left the area, moving across the border or into the real estate.

When to Go

There are three distinct **seasons** in the north of Phaic Tan. The Hot Season (Mar–May), the Rainy Season (June–Oct) and the Cease-fire Season (around New Year).

Shopping

Pha Phlung offers a wide range of shopping options, especially if you're on the look-out for aluminium urinals. Visitors can also pick up trinkets and **bric-a-brac** as well as antiques (which are basically trinkets and bric-a-brac manufactured prior to 1980).

In the larger cities such as Nham Pong you'll find **skilled artisans** producing an extraordinary range of hardware (both domestic and military).

Hill-tribe people are skilled craftsmen and their bamboo flutes (right) produce shrill, high pitched tones that are keenly sought after by musicians as well as those wanting a novel but **effective personal alarm**.

Nham Pong

At first sight Nham Pong appears to be a crowded settlement of ramshackle buildings and crowded, filthy streets. It is.

But while the city is not particularly **picturesque**, the capital Nham Pong does provide a useful stepping-off point for those planning to explore the natural beauty of the Pha Phlung region. For this reason the city some time ago declared itself '**Gateway to the Rainforest**' although, with the nearest patch of serious vegetation being a malarial jungle some 120km east, this has recently been modified to 'Gateway to the Gateway to the Rainforest'.

Nham Pong was originally built as a river city, carefully designed to sit along the banks of the Chugalong River. In 1937 this river was dammed upstream and Nham Pong now sits beside an extensive series of **muddy channels**. But this didn't hamper development and, over the last 50 odd years, Nham Pong has grown into an exciting, **vibrant centre**.

The city itself was once a treasure trove of **temples** and **shrines** and, while over the years many of these have fallen into disrepair or been converted into hip hotels, quite a few still remain such as the famous Wat Klang. Home to a large, rotund Chinese-style Buddha image, this magnificent sacred figurine attracts busloads of **pilgrims** each day who throw coins into its navel to make merit and, occasionally, win an **on-the-spot cash jackpot**.

Overlooking the city are the spectacular limestone ridges of **Mt Khon Phi**. Long considered sacred, this peak was once climbed in 911 AD by King Achutack who declared himself eternal ruler of all he surveyed, before unfurling a large prayer flag and being blown off the summit, never to be seen again. These days visitors to Nham Pong can still climb Mt Khon Phi and from the top not only is one is afforded an excellent view of the whole city, it also gets you away from the smell.

Philippe Writes...

Sunrise over rim of Mt Khon Phi is a wonderful sight but one often marred by the hordes of tourists jostling for position with their handi-cams. I find that by getting to the peak around 3am and leaving while it's still dark you can have the place to yourself.

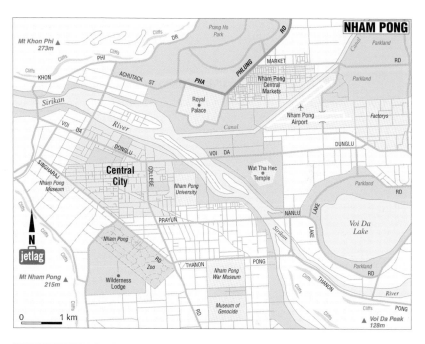

On days of national mourning in Nham Pong washing is often hung at half mast.

History

The origins of human settlement around Nham Pong are hard to determine but, as far as historians have been able to piece together, significant numbers of **nomadic Pah** peoples in China or Vietnam probably began migrating southward in small groups as early as the 4th century AD. From here they headed west up the **Hmok River** valley before spreading out across the plains to the north and then east, at which point they realized they were actually going in circles. (In fact, anthropologists mapping their movements have been known to get dizzy.)

The earliest known civilization to permanently move into the region was a tribe of primitive forest dwellers known as the **Kklar**. Unfortunately for these people they practised an unusual combination of vegetarianism and **cannibalism**, meaning the group soon died out from a combination of starvation and murder. The next ethnic majority to inhabit the area were the Vuhyen who arrived sometime round the 9th century. Keen traders, but somewhat lacking in business acumen, these people would gather local produce such as teak, rice, tea, gold and precious stones, and exchange it over the border for salt. In 873 AD the Vuhyen officially became the first hill tribe ever to go into **receivership**.

The original capital Xiong Kua was founded in 1068 by Huai tribes-people who were attracted by the site's location in a fertile river valley between two mountains. Several **small settlements** were built, only to be washed away each year by floodwaters, at which point the town was relocated to higher ground.

During the 14th century Nham Pong fell under the influence of rulers from the south and in 1388 the town became a **vassal state** of Bumpattabumpah city, although it kept its autonomy and own football team. Various battles for control of the capital were fought and in 1412 a young local Duya Nuk was proclaimed Queen. He was not happy with this new title and set about implementing a period of strict, authoritarian

Duya Nuk – the Shower Cap King

rule. For the next 40 years Nham Pong remained cut off from the outside world; schools were closed, primative books burnt and the people embroiled in a constant series of **bloody civil wars**. This is considered by many as the city's Great Period of Enlightenment.

In 1702 French forces massed on the city's outskirts in readiness to attack. Fearing the city was about to fall into enemy hands, Emperor Suhebarank gave a rousing speech in which he declared that it was better to die free than live as slaves. With this, the Emperor took a ceremonial sword and plunged it into his own heart, calling for his people to all do the same. Emperor Suhebarank was then stabbed over 10,000 times in a dramatic, if somewhat confused, show of loyalty.

By the time the French were finally driven out in 1890 Nham Pong was a **thriving commercial centre** with gemstones as its major export and the city remains famous for producing some of the world's most imperfect sapphires. Other semi-precious metals still traded today include tin, garnet and **depleted uranium**.

SMILE!

Visitors to Nham Pong often remark on the number of adolescent boys who are missing their front two teeth. These youths no doubt come from the Khaek tribal community where teeth are traditionally removed by the village shaman or high priest as part of an elaborate manhood ritual. Others may have come from a local nightclub.

Nham Pong's magnificent Wat Xiongkra (main photo) houses a series of remarkable murals (inset), many of which depict erotic episodes from The Ranayayan. *The Wat is open to the public and admission is $US2 per five minutes.*

Prang Ho

Prang Ho
A MAN AHEAD OF HIS TIME

Prang Ho is widely referred to as the **'Asian Da Vinci'**. Born in Nham Pong during the early 15th century, this prolific artist and visionary came up with many inventions.

The 'Coconut Catapult' was an ingenious strap and cog system that he hoped would be capable of raining coconuts on the enemy. Ho envisioned a protective wall of coconut plantations around the country.

His drawing of a rudimentary helicopter precedes Da Vinci's by many years and, while it is clearly un-aerodynamic, it did lead to the invention of the ceiling fan.

Much interest has centred on Ho's early sketches of what he described as a 'water horse', a vessel that pre-dates the modern jet ski by hundreds of years. Whilst primitive, Ho's water horse even appears to have an exhaust outlet designed to make it quiet.

 Amongst the many remarkable exhibits in the Prang Ho Museum are a set of blue-prints for a pre-fabricated pagoda, complete with a set of instructions and a 15th century Allen key.

A keen astronomer, Ho used a rudimentary telescope to postulate that the sun did not rotate around the earth but in fact both planetary bodies chased each other in a circle.

 Many scientists credit his steam-powered abacus as the being the world's first computer.

Ho is also credited with having made the first step towards the nuclear age in 1481 when he successfully split the coconut.

Tina Writes...

The bus trip north to Pha Phlung is said to be one of the most breath-taking trips in the world, passing along coastal cliffs and then through dense rainforests. So panoramic is the scenery that your driver will often point out sights of spectacular beauty along the way. On no account should you look out the window. The moment you do it's inevitable that a trained accomplice (posing as a fellow passenger) will be rifling through your hand luggage. I once travelled the entire stretch from Bumpattabumpah to Nham Pong without looking at a single scenic attraction. I arrived with no fond memories but my suitcase was safe.

Getting There

By Air

A new airline, Coconut Air, flies into Nham Pong (or, occasionally, into one of its surrounding hills) twice a week. Getting from the airport into town is quite easy as there are plenty of taxi drivers who will charge around 500p for the trip. Most of these drivers insist on **cash up front** – you pay and then they go to fetch their car, telling you to wait out the front. If you've agreed to this pre-paid arrangement, collect your luggage and then proceed to the **information booth** where you can report the fact you've just been robbed.

Customs regulations are quite strict and passengers flying in to Nham Pong Airport should remember that it is illegal to bring opium into the province; this is not an anti-drug measure but a **quarantine provision** to protect precious local crops from introduced disease or insect pests.

By Road

Pha Phlung was once regarded as one of the more remote and inaccessible provinces but thanks to the local **government's road building program**, combined with wide scale deforestation, it's now a lot easier to travel through by car. There are also **private buses** that wind their way through the steep countryside surrounding Nham Pong but these are slow and often delayed by landslides, rockslides and mud-slides as well as the company's insistence on employing **learner drivers**.

Getting Around

The easiest way to get round town is by cab, however, many Nham Pong taxi drivers and tuk-tuk owners have developed a **reputation for dishonesty**. Instead of taking you directly where you've asked to go they'll drag you off on a shopping tour of their 'favourite' shops and factories, pocketing a hefty commission on each of your purchases. Sadly this practice is spreading, with even accident victims reporting ambulances making several unscheduled stops at craft centres en route to the hospital.

There are also buses in Nham Pong but they're quite unreliable and most locals prefer to flag down a taxi or car-jack a passing vehicle.

DRIVING IN PHA PHLUNG

Instead of hopping on a bus many visitors prefer the convenience of driving themselves around Pha Phlung. While this option has its obvious merits, extreme care should be taken. Drug trading in the region is constant and fighting between rival factions often breaks out. Most towns have a sign on their outskirts indicating the likely risk level of armed hostility breaking out that day. If the sign indicates 'low' or 'medium' threat levels you should be fine to enter. If the sign reads 'high' or has been recently blasted away by an artillery shell, you might consider a detour.

A religious 'Peace Float' makes its way along the streets of Nham Pong. Shortly after this photo was taken, the float became involved in a road rage incident with another peace float and several monks were hospitalized.

Where to Stay

While a few backpacker joints exist downtown, most of the better hotels in Nham Pong tend to be clustered around picturesque Vang Duaq Lake. The lake itself is actually a large reservoir, formed by the controversial damming of the Prayun River further downstream and sometimes, late in the dry season, the drowned remains of old villages and environmental protestors can be seen sticking up out of the mud.

$$$ Expensive

✉ 33 Voi Da Donglu
☎ 32 569 479
@ nham@phoni.com.pt
🖃 DC MC V
    restaurant

The **Nham Pong International** Described as 'five floors of sheer luxury', this 25-storey hotel dominates the city skyline. Cheaper rooms can be found on the lower floors while the International's penthouse levels are popular with business travellers and snipers. The suites here are all large, decorated with genuine antique furnishings and expensive artworks although the presence of wall-mounted security video cameras in the bedroom does slightly detract from the atmosphere.

✉ 12 Voi Da Donglu
☎ 32 484 274
@ chao@phoni.com.pt
🖃 MC V

Chao Buri Originally built in 1925, a full refurbishment a few years back stripped most its charm (but sadly none of the asbestos) from this inner city hotel. Many rooms have balconies overlooking Vang Duaq Lake and in spring the views of its blue-green algal blooms are spectacular.

✉ 74 Prayun Nanlu
☎ 32 684 294
@ dong@phoni.com.pt
🖃 DC MC V
    pool

Luan Dong After closing down last year when its roof-top pool sprung a leak, the luxurious, if somewhat water-damaged Luan Dong is now back in business. Views vary depending on what room you get and are of either the lake, a shopping mall across the street or, at certain times of the day, the concierge's wife getting undressed. Facilities are good although the advertised 'access to nearby golf' does involve an overnight bus trip and border crossing.

Sven Writes... *For the Budget Traveller*

If you do decide to lash out and pay for a night in a decent hotel make sure you take full advantage of any complimentary goods provided. I never leave without a bag full of mini shampoo bottles, soap, tissues, hotel stationary, ashtrays, any unused toilet paper and of course the batteries from the TV remote control.

Nham Pong Villas Closer to the centre of town, this wonderful place features tiered shack-like bungalows hanging on to a hillside above the river, architecturally designed to look as if they're each sliding down the slope into the water. They are, so it's worth asking for an upper-level room.

✉ *63 Voi Da Donglu*
☎ *32 684 673*
@ *pong@phalti.com.pt*
▤ *DC MC V*

Wilderness Lodge For those wanting a taste of rainforest beauty without leaving the comfort of the city, Wilderness Lodge is the perfect option. Set in the middle of 50 hectares of artificial jungle, each of its rooms is decorated in wildlife motifs with genuine bear skin rugs and lamp shades made out of tiger skin. Guests used to be greeted in the lobby by tunes from a grand piano but ivory poachers broke in last year and stole the keys.

✉ *253 Thanon Pong*
▤ *DC MC*

$$ Mid-Range

Khao So Palace This reasonably priced resort just to the north of Nham Pong made news some years ago when local insurgents managed to infiltrate its heavily fortified perimeter by hiding in the back of a fresh linen truck. A major hostage drama was only narrowly averted when quick-thinking staff realized that the hotel's linen wasn't due to be changed for another six months.

✉ *53 Thanon Pong*
☎ *32 488 622*
@ *soso@phoni.com.pt*
▤ *V*

The Merkahn If you prefer staying a little out of town, consider a few nights at this authentic rural villa. Fashioned after a tribal long house, the Merkahn has been built with an eye for local detail, right down to the spear marks in its unpolished teak floors. Facilities are good although the Merkahn's pool can get a little crowded, especially round 4.00pm when local villagers drive their buffaloes down for a well-earned wallow.

✉ *426 Thanon Pong*
☎ *32 584 567*
@ *merkahn@phalti.com.pt*
▤ *DC V*
  topless check-in
  pool
  restaurant

PL Guest House One of the city's best family-run hotels, guests staying here will find all the comforts of home, such as unwashed dishes, stained carpets and a flatulent dog. The staff members speak little English but somehow can argue fluently in it.

✉ *163 Voi Da Donglu*
☎ *32 583 582*
▤ *DC*

$ Budget

⊠ 36 Prayun Nanlu
☎ 32 684 135
▱ DC MC
pool
gym
restaurant

Royal Trang House Closer to town, this comfortable hotel offers a good range of facilities such as restaurants, pools and a well-equipped fitness centre. There is no steam room as such but a couple of minutes waiting in the Trang's non air-conditioned lobby is just as invigorating. Rooms are a good size, provided you don't plan on standing upright, and all the balconies have excellent views, straight across to each other.

☎ 32 853 293
▱ DC MC V
guests sleep in somewhat-equipped courtesy van

Oriental Inn Renowned as one of the cheapest hotels in Nham Pong, guests booked into this budget establishment will be astonished when met at the airport in the hotel's very own courtesy van. This is where you will be sleeping.

⊠ 45 Prayun Nanlu

Tuck Mee Inn The quaintly named 'Tuck Mee Inn' is in fact owned by the Tuk Mee family and offers good, basic accommodation close to the city centre.

⊠ 163 Voi Da Donglu
☎ 32 583 582
▱ DC

Jimmy's Hotel Californian ex-pat, Jimmy Wade, set this place up in 60s and it didn't take long for it to become the hippest backpacker hang-out in Nham Pong. While the psychedelic decor and acid music remains, the hotel's wild reputation has been somewhat diminished since proprietor Jimmy's recent conversion to evangelical Christianity. Grace commences at 6.30. No double rooms. Cold showers only.

NOT FOR THE FAINT-HEARTED...!
A real delicacy in the hill country of Phaic Tan's north are deep-fried spiders. These critters, bred in special holes in the ground, are quite an interesting dining experience. They are best eaten by pulling the legs off one by one and sucking out the flesh. According to those brave enough to sample these creepy-crawly delights they taste a little like chicken, as do most exotic foods in Phaic Tan except for chicken which, curiously, tastes like beef.

Where to Eat

As a rule, northern cuisine is strongly influenced by the local people's long history of conflict, bloodshed and torture and many methods of interrogation have found their way into restaurant kitchens. Most meats are prepared (or 'softened up') by being slowly boiled, roasted over hot coals, bashed, stretched, deprived of sleep or simply wired up to a set of battery jumper leads.

When eating out in Nham Pong, the best advice is to follow the locals. If you head for a brightly lit, crowded place full of people eating and drinking then chances are you'll find yourself in a pretty good restaurant. Or a taxi.

Being somewhat isolated from the ocean Nham Pong is not a good place to order seafood unless you like your 'fresh fish' salted, pickled, dried or pork.

$$$ Expensive

Le Cochoun Perhaps the most authentic French bistro in town, they don't take bookings, the staff are uniformly off-hand (a sous chef was recently sacked for smiling at a customer) and there are always long queues of hungry hopefuls waiting out front to get a seat at one of the three tables. Le Couchon serves what they describe as a fusion of French and Phaic Tanese dishes, which basically amounts to very expensive rice.

✉ *112 Thanon Pong*
☎ *32 584 125*
▤ *DC MC V*

The Lakeside As its name suggest, this up-market eatery overlooks Vang Duaq Lake and serves a range of good meals. The most popular eating area is outdoors on the terrace and many diners round off their meal with a lake cruise, often inadvertently, when sections of the terrace floor collapse and float off across the water.

✉ *38 Voi Da Donglu*
☎ *32 435 641*
▤ *DC MC*
   outdoor dining

Hua Sing Each day executive chef Jimmy Sing scours the markets and stalls of Nham Pong, looking for ingredients that are fresh and in season. These are freighted to his brother's restaurant in Bumpattabumpah while the rest – wilted vegetables, stale bread and semi-rancid meats – are served in this busy downtown eatery.

✉ *87 Prayun Nanlu*
☎ *32 402 206*
▤ *MC V*

✉ *112 Thanon Pong*
☎ *32 485 693*
▭ *V*
   live music

Jester's This lively restaurant specializes in ethnic minority dishes. Guests sit cross-legged on cushions except for dessert which is traditionally eaten lying on your back. Upstairs is a mezzanine level overlooking the restaurant where a popular jazz band plays. They used to be four piece but, due to a lack of safety railings, are now a trio.

Philippe Writes...

When eating out, I always make a point of finding little, out-of-the-way places where the locals gather. Down a narrow back lane-way in Nham Pong I once found a small building with just a few tables where I sat myself down and said (in my best Phaic Tanese!) 'bring me the house special'. The atmosphere was so relaxed and authentic I could almost have been dining in someone's private house. As it turned out, I was. A genuine travel experience!

$$ Mid-Range

✉ *63 Prayun Nanlu*
☎ *32 589 001*
▭ *MC V*

Mei Too Part of a large, old colonial villa, walk into Me Too and you'll be greeted by comfortable armchairs, gleaming crystal, crisp linen and tastefully decorated table settings. Unfortunately, this is a ground floor homewares shop. The actual restaurant is upstairs in a dilapidated room overlooking the carpark.

✉ *82 Prayun Nanlu*
☎ *32 588 215*
▭ *MC V*

The Riverside Palace This year the River Side Inn officially became the Riverside Palace after it changed location to a larger venue and the owners bought a fridge. For such a big place the service is good, helped by efficient staff and the fact that daily specials are all prepared a week in advance. Freshly plucked ducks hanging from the window make for an exotic backdrop although a somewhat noisy one as many of the birds are still alive.

Traveller's Tip If you're after a quick snack after dark don't forget that Nham Pong has an extensive night food market where you can buy produce the owners weren't able to sell earlier at the day food market.

Tun Tun's Featuring candlelit chandeliers, huge incense sticks and mosquito coils hanging from the roof, this casual eatery would easily be the finest restaurant in Nham Pong, if it hadn't been extensively fire damaged last year.

✉ *93 Thanon Pong*
closed

Yuan Mi This tiny bistro tucked away in a back street is packed with diners just about every night. None of the staff speak English and the menus are all in Phaic Tanese so the best way to order is simply by pointing at what's on the table next to you. You'll either be served a sumptuous local delicacy or an overflowing ashtray.

✉ *75 Voi Da Donglu*
☎ *32 684 200*
▤ *DC V*

$ Budget

The Noodel Baahn Popular with backpackers and students, this casual eatery often gets so busy that during peak periods couples dining together may be required to sit on each other's lap.

✉ *14 Prayun Nanlu*
☎ *32 572 997*

Bistro Nham Pong Situated close to the centre of town, this friendly cafe offers a wide range of dishes, provided you like omelets. There's often music, if the chef turns his radio up.

✉ *30 Thanon Pong*
▤ *MC V*

Correction *In our last edition we described Bistro Nham Pong's rice wine cocktail as a real 'treat'. It is in fact a 'threat'.*

Kentuckee Fried Chicken Closely modeled on the US original, this home-grown boasts a recipe of '11 secret herbs and spices' although it's a fair guess that at least 10 of them involve chilli. All your KFC favourites are on the menu here except for the Zinger burger, which was removed after tests confirmed it contained traces of chicken.

✉ *61 Prayun Nanlu*
☎ *32 861 191*
▤ *DC MC V*

DRUG-FREE DINING
Without doubt a very special restaurant, **Cold Turkey** was set up to help train and rehabilitate many of Nham Pong's long-term opium users. Everyone here, from the head chef through to the drinks waiter, is a former addict now attempting to straighten out their lives. The menu is a little limited, due to the fact no knives or sharp implements are permitted in the kitchen and service can be a little erratic, especially around 'smoko' time, but you've got to admire the spirit behind this place.

Attractions

Wat Dha Hec This massive temple is situated on the banks of the Chugalong River and features a grand gilded entrance hall full of religious art. The ceiling is quite striking – literally – as tiles tend to fall off without notice, and construction helmets are recommended. The **Inner Temple** which, due to a design flaw, is located outside the main building, houses one of the most revered holy images in Phaic Tan, the **Jade Buddha**. This magnificent statue is said to have been carved from a single piece of jade although it's a little hard to know as it was knocked over and shattered by a cleaner some 50 odd years ago. The fully restored figurine now sits inside a glass cage high above the gold altar and is dressed in one of three costumes: a crown and jewellery for the spring season, a golden shawl in winter and a pair of cargo pants for the summer.

The **Phrap Yuam Chedi** sits on an elevated terrace overlooking the courtyard. It was built in 1655 to house a leg bone from the famed mystic Phrap Yuam, but this plan was never realized as Phrap Yuam was still alive and steadfastly refused to part with his limb.

The **Nham Pong National Museum** has a large collection of artifacts and treasures plundered from all over Southeast Asia. The ground floor is dedicated to temporary exhibitions such as *Combating Head Lice Through the Ages* while the second floor contains a fascinating array of ancient weaponry, well worth a visit even if many of these implements are missing, having been borrowed by local hill tribes keen to settle a border dispute. Also on display are sky rockets made by local farmers for the annual **Bun Bang Festival** in which huge gunpowder rockets are shot into the clouds to 'fertilize' them. Over the decades these have become even more elaborate and powerful, culminating last year in a three stage missile system that brought down the IndoStar-2 GEO satellite.

The **Nham Pong Adventure Centre** is situated on a bridge over the Chugalong River and is well worth a visit. Beware, however, bungee jumping is new to the province so it's fair to say it's going though a trial and error stage. Don't be surprised if the operators ask you to jump in a full scuba outfit.

Traveller's Tip

If you fall seriously ill during your stay in Phaic Tan, don't be alarmed. The main hospitals will treat Western Tourists and send charges directly to your travel insurance company. Beware, though, your policy may not cover faith healing.

The magnificent Inner Temple entrance at Wat Dha Hec. The collonade and roof structure were built by Emperor Duynak in 1655. The yellow doors were added by his great-great-great-great-great-grandson during a 1970s renovation.

For those with an interest in military history, **Nham Pong's War Museum** provides a graphic insight into the horrors of war. Visitors arriving will immediately be confronted by disturbing images of emaciated and often crippled figures in bloodstained uniforms. These are guides and will be happy to show you round for a small fee.

Next door is the equally popular **Museum of Genocide** which is also worth a visit. Those planning to see both might consider buying a Family Pass that gives you and the kids entry into the War Museum, the Museum of Genocide, the Mass Graves of Liqoc Qoch and the newly opened Torture World.

Situated on the peak of **Mt Khon Phi** is a large silver and jade Buddha, believed to have been built sometime during the 17th century. This gilded figure is particularly revered and, given its lofty position, can be seen from all directions except the south where it is obscured by advertising hoardings.

Traveller's Tip

Northern Phaic Tan has a long history of warfare during which its people lived under quite horrifying conditions, sheltering in cramped, airless bunkers. For a taste, you can either visit the Military Musuem or spend a night at the Nham Pong Youth Hostel.

Despite drawing large crowds, Nham Pong 'snake buskers' often struggle to make a living as spectators are rarely prepared to get close enough to leave a donation.

The Royal Palace

Dating from the 16th century when Phaic Tan's Royal Family would use this as their summer residence, the **Royal Palace of Nham Pong** (right) is well worth a visit. As you walk through the main gates you'll pass between two ornate **obelisks** that appear to be ancient carvings but are in fact cleverly disguised metal detectors, installed after a German backpacker was caught smuggling **silver roofing tiles** out in his shorts. From the entrance, begin on your left with a room of small ancient crafted ceramic artifacts. This is the ladies' toilet.

From here cross the courtyard and enter the main palace chamber – one of the largest **gilded halls** in the world (sunglasses may be rented). The floor of this hall is made out of 10,000 **gold tiles** that would make a dazzling sight if it wasn't for the fact it's covered in 10,000 carpet tiles.

At the back of the main hall you will find the **Royal Chamber** – considered the most important room in the Imperial Palace – as this was where the King received important dignitaries and heads of state. Less important visitors were received in the **garage**.

On the walls you will notice a large **tapestry**, made by **Prince Ferduk**, the eldest son of his Majesty King Tralanhng. Prince Ferduk is in fact a prolific artist and many of his works hang in public spaces, as does anyone foolish enough to criticize the young royal's somewhat **simplistic style**.

The second floor houses a collection of imperial clothing and silks, including robes once belonging to various members of the Royal Family. Of particular interest is a pair of **batik underpants** recently worn by Her Majesty Queen Suahm Luprang that hang from the ceiling and form a massive dividing curtain down the centre of the room.

If you're interested in seeing even more lavish adornments – Chinese porcelain, intricate silver work, **jewel-encrusted crowns** – then on your way out head over to the captain outside the Royal Barracks and ask him to open his mouth.

LUCKY IN LOVE

The Phaic Tanese are highly superstitious people and pretty much everyone wears some type of protective or lucky amulet. These come in many forms, mainly religious, although others are designed for more practical purposes, such as the very popular twin phallus donk charms often carried by local men. A set of these not only ensures sexual potency, they can also double as a handy set of chopsticks.

Phra Ramlee House This is the home where legendary Phaic Tanese actor, director, singer and composer V. Phre Ramlee was born and raised. A gallery of photos and personal memorabilia offers a unique glimpse into the life of this silver screen star but for a more direct experience head upstairs to his bedroom where the man himself is likely to be asleep. (Single women are advised against going alone.)

Nham Pong's famous **Night Market** used to be a major attraction but since authorities recently clamped down on counterfeit stalls it's lost its appeal, having been reduced to just three shops and an information booth. Better value is the Central Market, situated behind the Royal Palace. Open daily from very early until dusk, this market is a huge maze of shops selling just about any regional craft you can imagine. There's basket weaving for everything from place mats to beach umbrellas (yet, oddly, they don't do baskets) as well as sarongs, brass-ware pots and novelty beer mugs made out of discarded artillery shells.

In many Pha Phlung villages prophylactics are still handwoven.

Nham Pong Zoo For those seeking a bit of nature, this impressive open zoo has over 120 species of birds and animals, including deer, zebras and tigers. To reduce costs and minimize the chance of escape, most of the exhibits have been stuffed but they are all realistically displayed. The zoo also features one of the largest butterfly farms in the world, with over
4000 flying specimens in the one specially built glass jar with holes in the lid. One word of warning – the advertised '**animal-feeding shows**' actually involve little more than zoo staff having lunch.

Nham Pong University A respected seat of learning, this grand academic institution was the scene of violent student riots a few years back, led by a group of undergraduates enrolled in the Peace Studies program.

Praypok Palace Looking more like a Victorian mansion than a Phaic Tanese palace, this gawdy, three-storey teak structure was built in 1867 by a local businessman as a summer retreat. With its unusual combination of construction styles and materials (the roof is laminex), this place is best viewed at night when it can't be seen.

> **I SPY** The American CIA have had a long involvement in Pha Phlung, starting during the 1960s when a covert group was sent in to attempt to halt the drug trade. They were followed by another group who attempted to promote the drug trade in an effort to finance an insurgency, unaware that a third CIA group had been secretly inserted to back the counter-insurgency. A fourth and final group was then sent in just to figure out what was going on.

Friday is Outdoor Market day in Nham Pong when all food and produce is brought out of the supermarket, marked up by 20% and sold to westerners.

Philippe Writes...

I laugh at people who refuse to go trekking without a guide. For me, the only way to truly experience the splendour of the northern jungles is by deliberately getting lost. I once spent two weeks wandering in circles through the Wet Sok Mountains, dehydrated, covered in leeches and battling dysentery. This fortnight will live in my memory as yet another genuine travel experience.

Trekking

Many people visit Pha Phlung with the sole intention of going on a trek and this is certainly an excellent way of experiencing the region and its **unique inhabitants**. However, with the number of trekkers now averaging about six for every one villager you may be expected to queue for your unique glimpse at a person untouched by modern civilization. And despite **tour operators** claiming that they will take you to 'remote' or 'untouched' villages, it's a little hard to believe this when you're greeted by a community chief wearing a Van Halen T-shirt.

Sadly, some 'authentic' villages have become little more than **tacky souvenir centres** where visitors are forced to buy a certain amount of poor quality handicrafts before being allowed to leave. Due to excess tourism, these places have been turned into little more than human zoos and are best avoided although, if you do choose to visit, come around 2.30pm when the villagers are fed.

Choosing a Trekking Company

There are dozens of different outfits offering guided trips. The **tourist office** in Nham Pong has a list of those who meet minimum standards. Make sure your guide speaks at least some basic English and is qualified in first aid, navigation and **rapid fire pistol shooting**. It tends to be worth paying extra for a drug-free guide, especially if you plan trekking in a straight line.

How Long?

The length of your trip is another consideration. Operators offer **packages** ranging from those that last for an entire week through to ones that feel as if they do. As a general rule, you'll have a head guide and a team of porters. What usually happens is that the porters will leave with your gear at dawn. This is the last you are likely to see of them. Once new supplies and porters have been arranged you'll head off. Remember, porters expect to be tipped, the amount depending on how many kilos they've carried over what distance and for how long. You might have to add a few hundred p'ting if you want them to stop singing.

Correct clothing is essential. If trekking onto higher peaks make sure to carry a warm top and raincoat. Those trekking through opium growing districts might also consider tossing in a **bullet proof vest**. In environmentally sensitive areas it may even be necessary for trekkers to carry their own waste out. Brightly **embroidered shoulder bags** make the ideal container for this and can be purchased at any market.

STAYING IN A VILLAGE GUESTHOUSE

For many trekkers a highlight of their trip will be spending the night in a traditional village longhouse or *Li-kei*. Here you can experience authentic tribal life, sharing meals and daily activities with the people. Remember, even though you may be paying for the privilege you are still a guest of the hill tribes and when staying in a traditional village there are certain rules of etiquette to be observed.

Food and Drink When offered a meal or something to drink, it is considered extremely rude to refuse to it. If unsure, take a small portion and wait for your host to look away before tossing it to the dog. If this animal is still standing a few minutes later you should be safe to continue eating.

Photography Many of the people are highly superstitious and it is considered unlucky to be photographed without an up-front cash payment.

Music In the evening you may be treated to a musical performance in which everyone sits in a circle while the head villager plays a CD of tribal music. Try and look interested.

Darts Many villagers still use blow darts and if you're lucky you may get to witness a blow dart competition. These are generally held indoors, often at a tavern and, instead of shooting wild animals, competitors will attempt to hit a round board while holding a glass of beer.

Elephant trekking is also popular. Those trekking on a budget will often attempt to reduce costs by getting an entire family on the one animal.

Types of Treks

Deluxe Safaris A relative new-comer to the trekking scene, this Nham Pong-based company offers luxury five-day jungle trips catering to the top end of the market. The tour begins with a challenging walk, from your hotel room to the air-conditioned four-wheel drive that will take you deep into the hills. From here you're on foot but all gear is carried by porters who walk on ahead and make sure each camp is fully set up before clients arrive. Sumptuous meals are prepared every night by celebrity chefs choppered in for the occasion and tents all feature floorboards, heating and their own wine cellars. The highlight of the trip is spending a night in traditional village-style accommodation, re-modelled by spanish designer **Garcia Pez**, featuring minimalist white walls and **Poltronau Frau** furniture. Late in the night there's a performance of traditional dance, re-interpreted and choreographed by an avant-garde New York troupe.

Global Green Treks For those concerned about the possible impact of tourism on the fragile rainforest region, consider booking a trip with Global Green. This award-winning eco-tourism operation boasts environmental stewardship as a major part of their operation. Look for their glossy brochures littering the main street of Nham Pong.

The Hill Tribes

Apart from being a region of enormous natural beauty, the northern province of Pha Phlung is also home to Phaic Tan's many **hill tribes** whose cultures are dissolving rapidly in the face of modernization and tourism.

The word 'tribe' has poor connotations and is perhaps not the best term to describe the many **ethnic minorities** living in the north. In the Phaic Tanese language these people are more recently referred to as *humounga* or 'insurgents'. Whilst many still choose to live in isolated villages, you may be lucky enough to still catch a glimpse of these simple folk, stopping drivers on remote highways in their **traditional head dress**, the balaclava.

Visiting a hill tribe can be a wonderful experience and there are numerous treks available. For those less fit or pressed for time it is possible to arrange for a hill tribe to visit you, although advance notice should be given to your hotel so they can put some plastic sheeting down.

The nomadic Saiko people are such enthusiastic cigar smokers that they have developed a portable humidor, worn on the head.

To find out first-hand about Phaic Tan's many different hill tribes it's worth visiting the Ethnic Museum in Nham Pong. A lot of them work there as cleaners.

The Major Hill Tribes of Pha Phlung

The Huai These people form the largest single group in the north. They have been engaged in a long-running guerilla war against provincial authorities since about 1920. Their homes are typical of the area – bamboo shanties surrounded by razor wire – and the dominant religion is animism.

THE HUAI

The Khaek The second largest ethnic group in Pha Phlung, the Khaek have always been strongly associated with opium farming. As well as selling it as a cash crop, the people smoke opium themselves, so don't expect the buses to run on time. Married women wear brightly coloured, characteristically V-shaped, dresses while unmarried females in the village opt for low-cut denim hipsters.

THE KHAEK

The Khoak These people live in traditional houses (known as hide-outs) and practise slash-and-burn agriculture, an unavoidable consequence of ploughing heavily land-mined fields. The men wear plain indigo-dyed cotton shirts while the women adopt a more distinctive, eye-catching style of dress by walking around in bike shorts. The Khoak were the only group to have developed their own written language yet, sadly, never developed pencils so were unable to fully exploit the achievement.

THE KHOAK

The Saiko Like many of the other minorities, the Saiko are fond of heavy jewellery and will steal it at any opportunity. While the Saiko are predominantly Taoists, Irish catholic missionaries have also had an impact, with many of the villagers suffering from alcoholism. Older members of the tribe still speak an interesting local dialect, in which verbs are often replaced by a high-pitched giggle.

THE SAIKO

THE NANGA

The Nanga Largely inhabiting the lower valleys, the Nanga build elaborate wood and stone houses decorated with intricate teak carvings. Oddly, they are nomadic people and spend much of the year pulling these structures down and loading them into carts. Both men and women wear simple clothes along with a look of extreme fatigue.

The Paewa A nomadic people by tradition, the Paewa were once proud warriors who would behead enemies, a practice now outlawed in all circumstances except those involving theft of a motor vehicle.

THE TROK

The Trok Quiet, shy and peace-loving people, the Trok are strict Buddhists who long ago renounced any form of violence or warfare. The last surviving members died out many hundreds of years ago.

THE PAEWA

05

Phaic Tăn
Sukkondat

Introduction

Traditionally Phaic Tan's poorest region, due to the infertility of its soil, lack of natural resources and high number of casinos, the western province of Sukkondat still has much to recommend for the intrepid traveller prepared to look beyond its **bleak, granite plains** and **extensive swamplands**. While much of the region is flat and somewhat lacking in charm, there are pockets of great beauty and visitors here will certainly not be troubled by crowds. In fact, each year the province of Sukkondat receives less than 2% of the total number of visitors to Phaic Tan, a statistic that hasn't stopped its local Tourism Bureau declaring the province 'the place to be'.

Of course, poverty often breeds social unrest and over many years the people of Sukkondat have eagerly embraced any ideology offering a way of improving their lives. For decades the region was fertile ground for **communism**, followed by a surge of **Christian evangelism**. Nowadays the focus is on **Pilates**.

Historically, Sukkondat is the only region of Phaic Tan never to have been colonized; no foreign power has ever invaded the province, nor expressed the least interest in doing so.

Philippe Writes...

The moment I heard that Sukkondat province was hard to reach, under-developed and desolate I knew I would love it.

RELIGIOUS BELIEFS

Whilst primarily Buddhist, over the years the people of Sukkondat have absorbed a wide variety of religious influences including **Taoism**, **Animism**, **Hinduism** and **Sikhism**. Because of this the dominant religion throughout the province could best be described as **Confusionism**.

The capital of Sukkondat is the provincial centre of Sloh Phan. One of the lowest lying cities in the world, much of Sloh Phan is so far below sea level that bath tubs here take several days to drain. With its streets often flooded, much of the city is linked by an extensive series of rivers, canals, channels and **open drains** that the locals are particularly adept at negotiating in small row boats. Further afield there is much to see in Sukkondat, such as the majestic Khao Dung plains, a broad stretch of barren, arid tundra dotted with patches of scrub forest. It is here you can find the extraordinary *Roteh* orchid believed to be one of the largest flowers in the world. The *Roteh* blooms only once a year, its petals opening out to reveal a vile, unsightly, putrescent mass that is traditionally carried in a bouquet by Phaic Tanese brides.

Then there's the infamous border town of Gung Ho, a fascinating – if somewhat volatile – industrial centre full of **redneck charm**. A large arch appears over the main road as you approach welcoming you with the words – 'Gung Ho – Town of Harmony'. Several bodies usually hang from nooses beneath this arch, a potent warning for anyone thinking of skipping town without paying their hotel mini bar bill.

Traveller's Tip

Fighting often breaks out in Gung Ho between rival factions of gem merchants and before you head off it's worth checking with the Tourist Information Centre that there are no armed clashes taking place. If the Information Centre is on fire or under mortar attack it might be worth postponing your visit.

Traditional Sukkondati farmers still plough their fields in the time-honoured way – using illegal immigrants as cheap labour.

Sloh Phan

Despite its isolation, the provincial centre of Sloh Phan has developed into a large, dynamic city full of **unique attractions**. The Hanging Gardens of Tamboy, so named due to the large number of **public executions** held there, draw large numbers each year.

Then there's the Sloh Phan Museum of Modern Art, its walls adorned with the largest collection of abstract works in Asia. On weekends the Museum doubles as a **paint-ball venue**.

A deeply religious city, in the morning Sloh Phan monks can be seen walking the streets collecting food, alms or aluminium cans. Of course, many of the 'streets' are actually canals and the city is divided by an extensive series of waterways, the largest of which being the stately **Donkekong River**, home to the extremely rare Irrawaddy freshwater dolphins who can occasionally be seen swimming in its shallows. Fishing for, netting or spearing these dolphins is technically illegal but then, so is drink driving, and the chances of prosecution are remote.

For more details about Sloh Phan, visit the tourism board's Visitor Information Centre where you will find a wide range of literature and maps. There is also friendly staff although they are not permitted by law to answer any questions.

FISH FACT

Scientists have long wondered just how many dolphins live in the Donkekong River and in 2003 local authorities decided to commission a survey. Over several weeks various sections of the river were selectively netted, with the catch being carefully weighed, measured and deep-fried. Final figures have yet to be collated but interim results suggest that there are now 72 fewer dolphins than there were before the survey started.

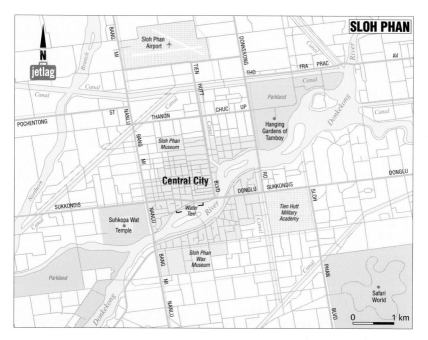

A group of renegade Sloh Phan monks march for the right to wear non-orange robes.

History

It is said that **King Lhomadhi** himself chose the site for Sloh Phan, possibly after a long night of drinking, and, in 527, decreed a settlement be built. Being made up largely of swampland and stagnant marshes, the first step was to drain the area, a task made difficult by the fact that the Phaic Tanese people had yet to master the basic principles of gravity.

After several years spent unsuccessfully attempting to run water up specially designed pipes the scheme had to be abandoned. Instead, landfill was brought in and slowly the town grew. Essentially a **trading post**, Sloh Phan is believed to be one of the first cities in the world to pioneer the art of making **pewter**. What should have been a major metallurgical breakthrough turned, however, to tragedy when the local people attempted to eat it.

By the 12th century Sloh Phan had developed as a gathering spot for various tribes who came here to trade, socialize, drink and fight – generally in that order. It was during this period that many of the city's most famous buildings were constructed, including the magnificent **Suhkopa Wat**. This ornate temple sits on the banks of the Donkekong River and, despite being surrounded by an astonishing succession of moats, fences, barricades, gates, doors and walled enclosures, has been broken into on over 7000 separate occasions.

In the 18th century the French finally took notice of Sloh Phan and sent a force to occupy the town. In 1789 French soldiers surrounded the city and an envoy was sent to **King Heuk Jong** demanding that all 100,000 of his troops lay down their arms. The savvy monarch boldly replied, 'How about 60,000?' The French then offered 75,000 but King Jong refused to budge and, several hours later, the French walked away with 70,000 and a free camera case.

Sukkondat locals will tell you that the 'Lost City of Hyung Fen' is a must-see attraction. Unfortunately, no one knows exactly where it is.

EASTERN AMAZONS

In the centre of Sloh Phan's main square (Bung Wohk) you will see an impressive statue of a woman wielding a large sword. Her name is Kquxi Proh and she is considered to be Phaic Tan's most famous and gifted female warrior. Born into a family of famous acrobats during the 14th century, Kquxi Proh dreamed of one day becoming an imperial guard. Unfortunately, her parents wanted her to become a hairdresser. So at the age of 10 she ran away from the circus to study combat under the famous sword master Lip Sipsuk. There she trained for several years until the death of her master from an infected paper cut. At the peak of her sword-fighting powers it was said that Kquxi Proh could defeat any man in the Royal Palace. Yet, oddly, she still needed help opening the lids on jars.

DID YOU KNOW?
When King Heuk Jong died in 1803, his son Prince Batahngor inherited the throne. His brother got the rest of the furniture.

Communications

Being so isolated, Sloh Phan was only recently connected to the country's national phone network. But even today this communication link is often severed when rogue logging contractors decide to clear-fell a line of poles holding up the telephone lines and sell them as firewood. But it's not all bad news and, after years of promises, Sloh Phan's first **internet café** was officially opened in 1998 by Prince Ferduk who, at a special ceremony, downloaded a picture of Jennifer Lopez in the nude.

Getting Around

Of course the best way to get around Sloh Phan is on board one of the many *thubs,* or small boats, that ply the **canal system**. For those using the roads you have a choice of Minivans as well as Demivans, which are basically minivans that have been involved in some sort of **head-on collision**.

Sven Writes...
For the Budget Traveller
Internet cafés are a great way of keeping in touch with family and friends back home but be warned – many places charge by the minute. To reduce costs I write one email and then send it to everyone on my address list. Sure, I'd prefer Mum didn't read about my latest sexual conquest but that sort of minor embarrassment is more than compensated for by the savings you can make.

Where to Stay

Visitors to Sloh Phan should remember that the city is only just beginning to build a tourist infrastructure. Up until now the only outsiders staying here were businessmen, diplomatic officials, aid agency staff and CIA operatives. Consequently, the range and standard of hotel accommodation available is still very limited. Amongst the options:

$$$ Expensive

✉ *33 Sukkondis Donglu*
☎ *35 283 623*
@ *sukk@phalti.com.pt*
🖬 *DC MC V*
  pool
  live music

The Royal Sloh Phan Undoubtedly *the* place to stay downtown, this is a great place from which to explore the city. The hotel is always abuzz with activity, whether it's visiting dignitaries or simply animal welfare agencies removing protected species from the lobby zoo. It boasts a large riverside pool and there are some fine dining options, although most will involve a flight to Bangkok. Rooms are priced according to their view of the city – the less you see, the more you can expect to pay.

✉ *153 Bang Mi Nanlu*
☎ *35 322 300*
@ *bhan@phoni.com.au*
🖬 *DC V*
  pool

The Bhanakam International This eight-storey hotel blocks some of the finest views in Sloh Phan. One of the city's most luxurious places to stay, the Bhanakam's outdoor pool complex was closed in 2002 after a major leptospirosis outbreak was traced to its spa. The aquatic facility has now been re-opened however, guests planning to swim are advised to use an antibiotic-based sunscreen.

✉ *183 Sukkondis Donglu*
☎ *35 643 034*
🖬 *V*

The Mata Hon An interesting addition to the city, the Mata Hon ranks as Phaic Tan's first and only Swiss Alpine themed hotel. Built in the style of a ski chalet, the Mata Hon features large rooms with open fireplaces and genuine bear skin rugs. Sitting back sipping a glass of gluwein you could almost believe you were in the European Alps, if it weren't for the mosquitoes, profusely sweaty staff and constant hum of 200 air-conditioning units set on high.

$$ Mid-Range

Hotel Chuc Nhu The general atmosphere here is marked by failing neon signs, peeling paint and worn carpets, an odd mix for a hotel that was only opened last year. The Chuc Nhu offers decent rooms at reasonable rates and even has several non-smoking rooms, although both of these are below ground.

✉ *62 Thanon Chuc Up*
☎ *35 349 293*
▤ *DC*

The Sloh Phan Inn Another basic accommodation option close to the city centre, the Sloh Phan Inn once boasted being the tallest hotel in the city. However, having being constructed on reclaimed swampland, this claim may have to be revised as there are now only two floors still above ground. Note – employees here are not paid a wage and survive solely on tips so it's not unusual for the housekeeping staff, having cleaned your room, to then throw themselves at your feet, sobbing and holding up photos of their 14 children. Don't be fooled.

✉ *6 Bang Mi Nanlu*
☎ *35 382 703*

The Imperial Inn A popular base for tourists, the Imperial was once a 17th century tea house, complete with ornate rooms and wide, spacious balconies. A few years back the place was bought and lovingly demolished by new owners who built this bland, mid-priced concrete edifice. Despite the changes, many rooms at the Imperial still exude an exotic air although mercifully this is largely disguised by the liberal use of pungent deodorizers.

✉ *211 Sukkondis*
☎ *35 221 641*
▤ *MC V*

Tina Writes...

Most hotels provide a small peephole in the door to allow guests to see who is outside but my advice is to be extremely wary about using these. I've heard of several people staying in so-called 'reputable' hotels who have looked through the peephole only to have a syringe full of anaesthetic pumped into their eye-ball. Several hours later they've woken up in a bath full of ice with a fresh abdominal scar and one less kidney.

$ Budget

✉ *6935 Sukkondis pool*

The Golden Bridge Hotel The Golden Bridge bills itself as a 'downtown resort', something of an overstatement for a two-star guesthouse some 27km from the city centre. But rooms are cheap and the staff not unfriendly. The hotel's large, badly leaking pool is re-filled with water each morning and can be enjoyed by swimmers until about lunchtime at which point it becomes a skate-boarding facility.

✉ *62 Thanon Chuc Up*
☎ *35 294 675*
▤ *MC V*

The Amajhaya Guesthouse Popular with backpackers and those on tight budgets, the Amajhaya is surprisingly clean and well maintained. Rooms are mopped daily – which is a pity, as most are carpeted – and the suites all feature luxurious woven rugs, as do the two owners, brothers who have clearly failed to come to terms with their own hair loss.

Sven Writes...

The cost of accommodation can quickly blow your holiday budget, especially in bigger cities, but here's a tip. Most railway stations have left luggage lockers and, if you're prepared to 'rough it' a little, it's possible to sleep inside one for a tenth of the cost of a hotel room. Don't forget to allow a few hours each morning for the bloodflow to return to your legs before heading off to enjoy the cash you've saved!

Sloh Phan is undergoing something of a construction boom, with new hotels and apartment blocks going up every few months. Due to substandard building techniques, this is often how long many of them will remain standing and visitors are advised against paying rent more than a week in advance.

Where to Eat

Most of Sloh Phan's best eateries are clustered along the riverfront and it's not hard to find a good restaurant. Meat is the staple dish here, cooked in the traditional *hmer* style where the animal is skinned, gutted, coated in chilli paste and immersed in boiling oil, coincidentally, the same process applies to anyone overheard making criticisms of the local mayor.

$$$ Expensive

Hotel Hoc With its linen tablecloths and crystal glassware, this elegant eatery is considered the place to eat in Sloh Phan. Owner Mr Hoc runs a tight ship and some diners have reported being a little disturbed by his treatment of junior staff, slapping, pinching and – on one occasion – attempting to drown a drinks waiter in the punch bowl. But the food is excellent, with much of the fish coming straight out of the nearby river, so you know it's both fresh and high in lead.

✉ *64 Thanon Chuc Up*
☎ *35 643 826*
▭ *DC MC V*

River House With a large, open-air balcony looking out over the river, this up-market bistro is the perfect place to settle back and watch the sun go down. There's an extensive menu and those unable to decide can order the River Platter, featuring a range of special dishes that they weren't able to sell in the last 72 hours.

✉ *52 Bang Mi Nanlu*
☎ *35 290 896*
▭ *DC MC*
 outdoor dining

FLOATING FOOD

Perhaps the ultimate way to enjoy a meal in Sloh Phan whilst getting to see something of the city is to book a dinner cruise on one of the many floating restaurants that ply their trade along the river. The dress code on most of these boats is quite strict, with gentlemen expected to wear life-jacket and tie while women are preferred in inflatable bikinis. One tip – if seated anywhere below decks make sure to ask for an ice bucket. Not only will this keep your wine cool, it will give you something to help bail with should the barge begin sinking.

✉ *128 Thanon Chuc Up*
☎ *35 602 678*
▤ *DC*

The Curry Train Obviously influenced by the Japanese sushi train concept, this popular eatery offers patrons the opportunity to sample individual bowls of curry brought past on a conveyor belt. But you'll have to be quick as it's based on the Japanese Bullet Train system and the food tends to travel past at an alarming rate.

$$ Mid-Range

✉ *92 Bang Mi Nanlu*
▤ *DC MC V*

Sohm To Popular with locals as well as visitors seeking an authentic dining experience, Sohm To is a traditional restaurant where patrons sit on the floor and food is eaten with the hands – not always easy as they mainly serve soup.

✉ *49 Thanon Chuc Up*
☎ *35 299 454*
▤ *MC*

Patuxyoh Café This no-frills river-front eatery offers basic, hot curries and spicy stirfries with prices that won't burn a hole in your wallet. Unfortunately the same cannot be said for your oesophagus.

✉ *30 Thanon Chuc Up*
☎ *35 293 677*

Bella Italia! The sign on the front door proudly declares that chef Ziou Guak worked in Rome for eight years. What it doesn't tell you is that he worked as a petrol-station attendant. Nonetheless, the food is cheap and the bistro's low lighting not only sets a romantic mood, it also prevents you from spotting the cockroaches.

✉ *51 Sukkondis Donglu*
☎ *35 275 838*
▤ *DC MC*

The Taj Mahal Another ethnic eatery in the centre of town, the Taj Mahal features a striking white near-eastern decor. Inside you'll find Hindu carvings and on weekends a resident sitar player entertains. Strangely, they only serve Mexican food.

HOT STUFF!
You won't be in Sloh Phan long before coming across the unique taste of *nuok nam*, a food seasoning used extensively throughout the western province. *Nuok nam*, or fish sauce, is made by packing carp into jars between layers of salt and letting it all ferment. The resulting brine can then be used as nutritious seasoning or to strip paint. Several farming communities also use it as a deodorant.

$ Budget

Bistro Sen Hon Boasting an extensive western menu, diners are invited to name their favourite dish – lasagna, pizza, burgers – and watch the chef turn it into a stirfry. Sen Hon is a good spot to relax and beat the heat, unless you happen to score a seat next to the kitchen in which case it's an absolute sauna.

✉ *87 Bang Mi Nanlu*
☎ *35 294 451*

Do Rhon Rhon This laid-back bistro describes itself as having a 'tropical' ambience, meaning you should bring plenty of mosquito repellant. A good place to relax over a light meal or coffee, it's also not bad for kids as there's a petting zoo next door where the little ones can meet what you're about to eat.

✉ *104 Sukkondis Donglu*

Café Khocmay Many visitors say that the best thing about Café Khocmay is its view. That the restaurant is down a narrow lane-way surrounded by office towers might provide some clue as to the standard of food. Still, it's cheap and open everyday except Tuesdays when there's often a death in the kitchen.

✉ *66b Thanon Chuc Up*
☎ *35 193 699*
closed Tuesday

Sikyam Su Once one of Sloh Phan's most popular eateries, standards have slipped a little at this inner city eatery. For example, the 'Trio of Dips' now involves one bowl of watered-down ketchup. Service, too, can be a little erratic – one diner reported having her ashtray re-filled.

✉ *34 Bang Mi Nanlu*
☎ *35 284 120*
▭ *DC*

Correction *In our last edition we reviewed Sloh Phan's Bistro Thungwai, noting that 'the chef specializes in light meals'. This should of course have read 'the chef specializes in light metals'.*

DRINK UP!

The local brew in these parts is *Kak Qip Chau*, a sweet rice brandy that is traditionally ingested late at night when the drinker is feeling morose or depressed. Indeed, many bars in Sloh Phan have an 'Unhappy Hour', usually between 2 and 3am.

Attractions

The Sloh Phan Museum This massive red sandstone edifice holds an impressive collection of historical artifacts, tracing the city's development from the Stone Age and Iron Age through to the contemporary period, known officially as the Asbestos Age.

The Sloh Phan Wax Museum On a slightly less cultural note, Sloh Phan's wax museum was opened in 1982 with high hopes that it would provide a major tourist attraction. Sadly, due to inadequate air-conditioning, most of the exhibits have melted somewhat and it is almost impossible to tell who each figure is meant to represent, although a helpful sign at the base of each one offers some assistance.

Sloh Phan is home to Phaic Tan's largest Military Academy, the **Tien Hutt**, where all members of the country's armed forces come to receive basic training. The Academy received some unfortunate press a few years back when an officer based there went AWOL, hi-jacking a tank and heading into town where he got drunk and exposed himself to several tourists. Even though the soldier was court martialed and stripped of his rank as Army Chaplain, many Sloh Phan residents still resent the Academy's presence.

The magnificent Kampstuhl Palace was built in 1545 by Emperor Dhukaeng who lived here for 60 years, fighting off attacks from a variety of foreign invaders before eventually being forced out by rising land taxes.

ECONOMIC GENIUS

Widely regarded the 'Father of Duty Free Shopping', Sloh Phan-born Tho Fra Prac is arguably Phaic Tan's most famous economist. Prac attended Columbia University during the 1950s where, due to an interest in Keynes and Friedman, he studied for an MBA. Unfortunately, he failed, due to a stronger interest in girls and beer. It was while paying customs charges at Phlat Chat Airport that Prac had his remarkable epiphany, a breakthrough that led – not only to the invention of the 1 litre scotch bottle, the perfume miniature pack and a larger style of cigarette carton – but also to a lifetime study of bargain shopping. His brilliant research paper 'Economic Efficiencies Through Crafty Bargaining' formulated the first ever pricing model that accounted for hand gestures.

Prac's Postulate

pp (price paid) $=$ ep (expected price) $\div$ vr (vendor resistance) x Ch (histrionic co-efficient)

Outside the Museum you will see a large copper statue of **Pria Pochentong** (1912–78). One of Sloh Phan's most famous former sons, this visionary changed the face of eating out forever in 1953 when he invented the Lazy Susan. Pochentong is currently buried in Sloh Phan's main cemetery and every year on the anniversary of his death locals visit his grave and pay homage by spinning his revolving headstone.

The Academy of Dance The province of Sukkondat has a rich artistic heritage and much of this is celebrated in the region's traditional dance, performances of which are held here daily. Authentic (folk) dancing is at once captivating and sublime. It generally involves performers in traditional costume striking a series of highly stylized poses which they then hold, sometimes for up to 40 minutes at a time. There is no music, although a heavy drum is used to count time and mask the sound of people snoring.

Further Afield…

The Silver Pagoda This glittery temple is considered a little ostentatious by some more traditional lovers of religious architecture who question the spiritual integrity of a shrine boasting its own mirror-ball. But many of the Pagoda's older buildings present a more muted style. The main shrine was once covered in fine carvings – it is now covered in advertising hoardings.

Not far out of Sloh Phan you'll find **Safari World**, a popular 200ha car-safari park. Visitors here can drive up to and, in some cases, over the top of, more than 200 separate animal species.

The Sesak Caves Set in the side of a steep sandstone cliff-face, these caves are home to the tiny *miku* bat, believed by many local scientists to be one of the world's smallest and tastiest mammals. Inside the caves you'll find some natural thermal springs that are said to have therapeutic qualities. Many people suffering from dermatological conditions who have bathed here report that they no longer have skin problems. In fact, they no longer have skin as the water averages about 97 degrees celcius.

Although the **Donkekong River** flows through Sloh Phan at a fairly slow pace, some 20km upstream this same river provides one of the best **whitewater rafting** trips in Southeast Asia. The rapids here are Grade 4 level, as are unfortunately most of the river guides, so make sure you hold out for an adult. Whilst rafting the Donkekong remains a popular activity there has been some concern over high injury rates; rest assured that the rafting itself is relatively safe, it's just local tribesmen firing blow-darts that has tended to push the death toll up.

Correction *In our previous edition we described the Donkekong river as a 'broad waterway'. This should, in fact, have read 'bronze waterway', a product of un-regulated copper mining upstream.*

Lunchtime diners enjoy a meal at Rhamee's, named after local identity Rhamee Sukitra who is considered the best chef in town. Unfortunately he has never worked there.

A Sukkondat soldier takes a break from digging latrines to prepare breakfast.

In Phaic Tan it is generally wise not to share drink bottles.

A group of locals play bang meow, *a popular board game taken so seriously in Sukkondat that an independent referee/peace-keeper must watch on in case a minor dispute escalates into serious violence.*

The people of Phaic Tan welcome visitors
with this traditional greeting...

Come with Open Mind

Stay with Open Heart

Depart with No More
than 1.5 litres of
Duty Free Spirits.

Index

Due to numerological edicts, the following page numbers may not be entirely accurate.

Appendix A Phaic Tanese Lucky Numbers

Extremely Lucky

12, 57, 4189

Lucky

2, 5, 7, 11, 15, 17, 19, 25, 29, 51, 41, 45, 47, 55, 59, 71, 77, 71, 75, 79, 85, 89, 97, 101, 105, 107, 109, 115, 127, 151, 157, 159, 149, 151, 157, 175, 177, 175, 179, 181, 191, 195, 197, 199, 211, 225, 227, 229, 255, 259, 241, 251, 257, 275, 279, 271, 277, 281, 285, 295, 401, 409, 419, 421, 451, 455, 459, 445, 449, 457, 471, 475, 477, 479, 487, 491, 499, 505, 509, 521, 525, 541, 547, 557, 575, 579, 571, 577, 587, 595, 599, 701, 709, 719, 727, 755, 759, 745, 751, 757, 771, 779, 775, 787, 797, 809, 811, 821, 825, 827, 829, 859, 855, 857, 859, 875, 877, 881, 885, 887, 907, 911, 919, 929, 957, 941, 947, 955, 977, 971, 977, 985, 991, 997, 1009, 1015, 1019, 1021, 1051, 1055, 1059, 1049, 1051, 1071, 1075, 1079, 1087, 1091, 1095, 1097, 1105, 1109, 1117, 1125, 1129, 1151, 1155, 1175, 1171, 1181, 1187, 1195, 1201, 1215, 1217, 1225, 1229, 1251, 1257, 1249, 1259, 1277, 1279, 1285, 1289, 1291, 1297, 1501, 1505, 1507, 1519, 1521, 1527, 1571, 1577, 1575, 1581, 1599, 1409, 1425, 1427, 1429, 1455, 1459, 1447, 1451, 1455, 1459, 1471, 1481, 1485, 1487, 1489, 1495, 1499, 1511, 1525, 1551, 1545, 1549, 1555, 1559, 1577, 1571, 1579, 1585, 1597, 1701, 1707, 1709, 1715, 1719, 1721, 1727, 1757, 1757, 1775, 1777, 1779, 1795, 1797, 1799, 1709, 1721, 1725, 1755, 1741, 1747, 1755, 1759, 1777, 1785, 1787, 1789, 1801, 1811, 1825, 1851, 1847, 1871, 1877, 1871, 1875, 1877, 1879, 1889, 1901, 1907, 1915, 1951, 1955, 1949, 1951, 1975, 1979, 1987, 1995, 1997, 1999, 2005, 2011, 2017, 2027, 2029, 2059, 2055, 2075, 2079, 2081, 2085, 2087, 2089, 2099, 2111, 2215, 2221, 2257, 2259, 2245, 2251, 2277, 2279, 2275, 2281, 2287, 2295, 2297, 2509, 2511, 2555, 2559, 2541, 2547, 2551, 2557, 2571, 2577, 2581, 2585, 2589, 2595, 2599, 2411, 2417, 2425, 2457, 2441, 2447, 2459, 2477, 2475, 2477, 2505, 2521, 2551, 2559, 2545, 2549, 2759, 2775, 2771, 2777, 2785, 2787, 2789, 2795, 2799, 2707, 2711, 2715, 2719, 2729, 2751, 2741, 2749, 2755, 2777, 2777, 2789, 2791, 2797, 2801, 2805, 2819, 2855, 2857, 2845, 2851, 2857, 2871, 2879, 2887, 2897, 2905, 2909, 2917, 2927, 2959, 2955, 2957, 2975, 2979, 2971, 2999, 4001, 4005, 4007, 4015, 4019, 4021, 4027, 4049, 4051, 4057, 4075, 4079, 4091, 4095, 4099, 4111, 4127, 4129, 4155, 4159, 4155, 4157, 4159, 4177, 4201, 4211, 4217, 4219, 4229, 4251, 4241, 4245, 4255, 4259, 4271, 4271, 4275, 4285, 4289, 4297, 4527, 4557, 4559, 4549, 4557, 4575, 4575, 4591, 4597, 4409, 4421, 4425, 4441, 4447, 4451, 4457, 4475, 4481, 4485, 4495, 4507, 4515, 4517, 4519, 4525, 4547, 4549, 4571, 4577, 4585, 4591, 4597, 4705, 4721, 4757, 4759, 4745, 4749, 4751, 4757, 4775, 4775, 4779, 4791, 4705, 4721, 4725, 4729, 4755, 4751, 4759, 4785, 4787, 4789, 4795, 4799, 4801, 4815, 4817, 4851, 4871, 4871, 4877, 4889, 4905, 4909, 4919, 4951, 4955, 4957, 4945, 4951, 4957, 4977, 4979, 4975, 4987, 4999, 5001, 5187, 5191, 5205, 5209, 5217, 5221, 5229, 5251, 5255, 5257, 5259, 5271, 5299, 5501, 5507, 5515, 5519, 5525, 5529, 5551, 5545, 5547, 5559, 5571, 5571, 5575, 5589, 5591, 5407, 5415, 5455, 5449, 5457, 5471, 5475, 5477, 5479, 5491, 5499, 5511, 5517, 5527, 5529, 5555, 5559, 5541, 5547, 5557, 5559, 5571, 5581, 5585, 5595, 5707, 5715, 5717, 5725, 5751, 5757, 5745, 5759, 5771, 5775, 5777, 5791, 5797, 5701, 5709, 5719, 5727, 5755, 5759, 5771, 5777, 5779, 5779, 5795, 5797, 5805, 5821, 5825, 5855, 5847, 5851, 5855, 5875, 5877, 5881, 5889, 5907, 5911, 5917, 5919, 5925, 5929, 5951, 5945, 5947, 5977, 5989

Mildly Auspicious

4993

Unlucky

3, 6

PHAIC TAN
CUSTOMS

Department of Immigration
Phaic Tan Customs Service

Customs Declaration

Each arriving traveller (*or guardian/parole officer*) must provide the following information.

1. Family **Name**

   First (*given*)

2. **Birth Date** (*please do not include past lives*)

3. Place where you will be spending
   most time (*do not include hospitals*)

4. Date **Passport** issued/forged

5. **Countries visited** on this trip
   prior to Phaic Tan arrival

   Which one did you enjoy most?

   And why?

6. **Place of embarkation**

7. **Place you arrived**

8. **Place your luggage arrived**

9. The **primary purpose** of this trip is (*circle one*)

   • Business Vacation   • Drug Running   • International Witness Protection Scheme

   • Just need some time out to get my head together and prove I can survive without David

10. **I am (We are) bringing**

		Yes	No
a) Fruit, plants, food, insects		Yes	No
b) Meat, animals, animal/wildlife products		Yes	No
c) Bomb-making equipment (*other than for personal use*)		Yes	No
d) One of those singing bass fish you hang on the wall		Yes	No
e) Pornographic magazines or photos (*although digitally enhanced*		Yes	No

    shots of Hollywood celebrities pasted onto nude bodies are okay)

11. I have (We have) been in **close proximity** (*such as handling or fondling*) of **livestock**.

12. Are you or have you ever been a member of:

	Yes	No
a) the Nazi Party	Yes	No
b) the Khmer Rouge	Yes	No
c) AlQaeda	Yes	No
d) Rotary International	Yes	No

**I (WE) DECLARE THAT DURING MY STAY IN PHAIC TAN I WILL NOT MAKE ANY COMMENT THAT IS DEEMED
OFFENSIVE TO THE ROYAL FAMILY, ESPECIALLY RELATING TO THE QUEEN AND HER AMPLE GIRTH.**

(*Signature*)

*The Phaic Tan Customs Service is responsible for protecting the country against the illegal importation
of prohibited items. Customs Officers have the authority to question you and to examine your personal
property however this may be avoided through a small cash payment. If you are one of the travellers
selected for an examination, you will be treated in a courteous, professional and dignified manner until
we get your pants off at which point anything goes.*

220975 (17/05)

Other titles available soon
in the Jetlag Travel Guide series...

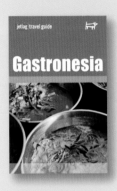

Costa Del Pom

Boasting 4 continuous miles of unspoilt English pubs, this is Europe's hottest and most congested summer destination. Enjoy sun, sea and unsatisfying sex on the beaches of Los Toplez, where most high-rise hotels feature 180 degree views of the hotel in front of them. Come on – turn a darker shade of pink on Iberia's party coast!

Pfaffländ

From the sterile cleanliness of Volvenhaagen to the orthopaedic footpaths of Birkenstockholm, this sub-arctic wonderland provides a smorgasboard of Nordic delights. Take a fauna and sauna safari through its pristine pine forests or if clubbing is more your scene then head to the seal colonies of Cløbberländ. In a land of 24-hour sunshine the days in this ice-encrusted country will somehow feel longer.

Gastronesia

Spread over 200 islands of the Qic Pù Peninsula, this forgotten jewel is fast re-emerging as one of Asia's hottest destinations. Known by lovers of spicy cuisine as the Scorched Palate Archipelago, visiting diners have been known to drown in their own sweat.

Sherpastan

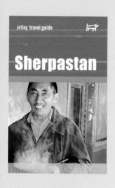

Sherpastan

From the moment you touch down in the high altitude capital of Oedema, this mountain kingdom will take your breath away. Try an ice trek across the Frostbittaan plains or, for the truly intrepid traveller, rent a guide and attempt an ascent of Mt Ingcosts.

Cartelombia

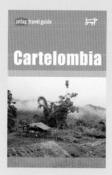

Cartelombia

Nestled at the foot of South America's rugged Cocainia Mountains, this former Spanish colony is at last making its mark on the world stage. From its bustling capital of Assassinaçion City to the remote jungle outpost of Pichapochetchu, this country is worth every bit of the effort and ransom required.

PLUS

Travel for Germans

JETLAG'S TITLE OF THE MONTH

In addition look out for these Specialist Jetlag Travel Guides

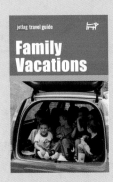

Family Vacations

For those planning a big trip with little ones, this guide features a wealth of handy tips. What's the best legal sedative for use on long bus rides? How can I cut airline ticket costs by checking infants on as unaccompanied baggage? Featuring a complete list of every McDonalds in the world along with instructions on how to say 'my child has an ear infection' in over 500 different languages.

Cycling the World

Don't even think of pushing a pedal without this book! Featuring detailed guides to the Top 5 flattest countries in the world plus a list of must-see international sites ranked according to gradient. All this plus pages of unnecessary but stylish accessories that will make you look good no matter how sore your arse is. Comes in a special, limited edition lycra cover.

Hair Raising Drives

From the spectacular Amafia Coast, featuring the most unfenced bends in Europe, to the unpoliced autobahns of San Mercedes, this guide covers the world's best auto routes at reckless speed. Packed with tips on insurance, drink-driving, speed limits and what to do in the event of side-swiping a local pedestrian, this book will get you into first gear. Comes with its own fold-out sick bag.